M000306145

Classic Day Walks in England & Wales

20 OF THE UK'S BEST WALKS

Vertebrate Publishing, Sheffield
www.**v-publishing**.co.uk

Classic Day Walks in England & Wales

20 OF THE UK'S BEST WALKS

Edited by
Jon Barton

Classic Day Walks in England & Wales

20 OF THE UK'S BEST WALKS

 First published in 2021 by Vertebrate Publishing.

Vertebrate Publishing, Omega Court, 352 Cemetery Road,
Sheffield S11 8FT, United Kingdom.
www.**v-publishing**.co.uk

Copyright © Jon Barton and the contributors 2021.
Page v constitutes a continuation of the copyright information.
Introduction copyright © Jon Barton 2021.

Jon Barton and the contributors have asserted their rights under the Copyright, Designs
and Patents Act 1988 to be identified as editor of and contributors to this work.

A CIP catalogue record for this book is available from the British Library.

ISBN 978-1-83981-069-5

Front cover: **Curbar Edge looking towards Froggatt Edge** *(Peak District),* **by Adam Long**.
Back cover: **Great Langdale seen from above Chapel Stile** *(Lake District),* **by Stephen Goodwin**.
All photography individually credited.

 All maps reproduced by permission of Ordnance Survey on
behalf of The Controller of Her Majesty's Stationery Office.
© Crown Copyright. 100025218.

Design by Jane Beagley, production by Cameron Bonser.
www.v-publishing.co.uk

Printed and bound in Europe by Pulsio.

Vertebrate Publishing is committed to printing on paper from sustainable sources.

Contents

* Shortcut available

Northern England

Southern England

Wales

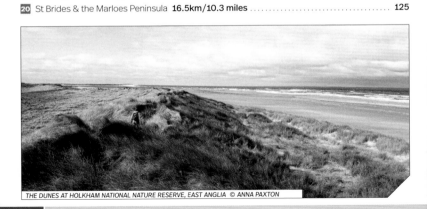

THE DUNES AT HOLKHAM NATIONAL NATURE RESERVE, EAST ANGLIA © ANNA PAXTON

**Classic Day Walks
in England & Wales**

AREA MAP & ROUTE FINDER

VIEW OVER THE COLLEGE VALLEY, NORTHUMBERLAND © DAVID WILSON

Introduction

Since the very first book in the Day Walks series, *Day Walks in the Peak District: 20 classic circular routes*, was published in 2005, the series has grown to cover the best walking country in England and Wales.

We asked each of the Day Walks authors to pick their favourite walk, so you can be sure that these walks really capture the feel of a particular area, or take you to an unexpected, quiet corner away from the crowds. We explore beaches and nature reserves in Norfolk with Anna Paxton, traverse the site of the Battle of Hastings with Deirdre Huston and take a take a hike up the quieter side of Moel Siabod in Snowdonia with Tom Hutton. Meanwhile, David Wilson shows us the highlights of Hadrian's Wall, Stephen Goodwin takes us on a stunning loop around Langdale in the Lake District and we explore the industrial archaeology of the Peak District with Norman Taylor and Barry Pope.

The authors of the Day Walks books are the most important part of the success of the series; we ensure that they are knowledgeable and enthusiastic about the areas that they write about. Most often they are local to the area and can draw on years of hiking in the landscape to design the best walks for someone new to the area to enjoy. Discovering a new area is much more interesting and rewarding for a walker if they are provided with some context and historical background to the landscape they are traversing.

We are so lucky in England and Wales to have such an array of exciting and beautiful places to explore on our doorstep – I hope this book will encourage you to get out there, guidebook and map in hand, and enjoy discovering somewhere new.

Jon Barton

Navigation

England and Wales are covered in full by a number of Ordnance Survey (OS) Explorer 1:25,000 or OS Landranger 1:50,000 maps. While the route descriptions and maps provided in this book give detailed information on the walks, carrying a separate map (along with a compass) provides you with a fuller picture of the surrounding area, and can be useful if you need to find an alternative route.

GPS and mobile phones

A GPS device is always useful. If this is on a mobile phone carry a powerpack to prevent the battery from going flat. Smartphones are particularly useful if an emergency arises as it can aid rescuers in locating the phone's position if a signal is present. Much of England and Wales has good phone signal coverage but there are always blind spots. If you need to make a call, try and get to high ground for a signal.

Walk times

Walk times are approximate; allow extra time for breaks and to explore places of interest along the way. If a walk goes off path across moorland this can add time; in winter always allow extra time.

Safety

Before beginning any of these walks it is important to ensure you are fully prepared for changeable conditions both in terms of weather and underfoot. Having the correct clothing and equipment is crucial, and you should always be fully prepared for any adverse or emergency situations. Leave details of your route with a person who knows what to do if you have not returned by a certain time. Beware of ticks and carry a removal tool. Always seek medical advice if you think you have been bitten.

RESCUE

In case of an emergency dial **999** and ask for **Police** and then **Mountain Rescue**. Where possible give a six-figure grid reference of your location or that of your casualty. If you don't have mobile reception try to attract the attention of others nearby. The standard distress signal is six short blasts on a whistle every minute.

EMERGENCY RESCUE BY SMS TEXT

In the UK you can also contact the emergency services by SMS text – useful if you have low battery or intermittent signal. You need to register your phone first by

texting '**register**' to **999** and then following the instructions in the reply. **Do it now** – it could save yours or someone else's life. **www.emergencysms.net**

The Countryside Code

See **www.gov.uk/government/publications/the-countryside-code** for more details.

RESPECT OTHER PEOPLE
» Consider the local community and other people enjoying the outdoors
» Park carefully so access to gateways and driveways is clear
» Leave gates and property as you find them
» Follow paths but give way to others where it's narrow

PROTECT THE NATURAL ENVIRONMENT
» Leave no trace of your visit, take all your litter home
» Don't have BBQs or fires
» Keep dogs under effective control
» Dog poo – bag it and bin it

ENJOY THE OUTDOORS
» Plan ahead, check what facilities are open, be prepared
» Follow advice and local signs

How to use this book

This book should provide you with all the information you need for an enjoyable, trouble-free and successful walk. The following tips should help:
» We strongly recommend that you invest in the relevant OS map (details in each route) for the walk in case you need to cut short the walk or take an alternative route.
» Choose your route carefully taking into account the time available, abilities and experience of all those in your group, and weather forecast – read the safety section of this guidebook.
» We recommend that you study the route description carefully before setting off. Cross-reference this with your map so that you've got a good sense of general orientation in case you need an escape route. Make sure that you are familiar with the symbols used on the maps.
» Get out there and get walking!

Maps, descriptions, distances

While every effort has been made to maintain accuracy within the maps and descriptions in this guidebook, we have had to process a vast amount of information and we are unable to guarantee that every single detail is correct. Please exercise caution if a direction appears at odds with the route on the map. If in doubt, a comparison between the route, the description and a quick cross-reference with your map (along with a bit of common sense) should help ensure that you're on the right track.

Note that distances have been measured off the map, and map distances rarely coincide 100 per cent with distances on the ground. Please treat stated distances as a guideline only. Ordnance Survey maps are the most commonly used, are easy to read and many people are happy using them. If you're not familiar with OS maps and are unsure of what the symbols mean, you can download a free OS 1:25,000 map legend from **www.ordnancesurvey.co.uk**

Here are a few of the symbols and abbreviations we use on the maps and in our directions:

ROUTE STARTING POINT	SHORTCUT	ROUTE MARKER	OPTIONAL ROUTE	ADDITIONAL GRID LINE NUMBERS TO AID NAVIGATION

KM/MILE CONVERSION CHART

Metric to Imperial
1 kilometre [km]	1,000 m	0.6214 mile
1 metre [m]	100 cm	1.0936 yd
1 centimetre [cm]	10 mm	0.3937 in
1 millimetre [mm]		0.03937 in

Imperial to Metric
1 mile	1,760 yd	1.6093 km
1 yard [yd]	3 ft	0.9144 m
1 foot [ft]	12 in	0.3048 m
1 inch [in]		2.54 cm

EDALE AND GRINDSBROOK CLOUGH, PEAK DISTRICT © JOHN COEFIELD

Section 1

Northern England

Whatever type of walking you prefer, Northern England has it all. Explore sand dunes and a nature reserve on Northumberland's stunning coastline, enjoy a hike on Lakeland fells, appreciate woodland colours in a quiet corner of the South Pennines or traverse high-level paths on the gritstone edges of the Peak District – you're sure to find something to tempt you to visit somewhere new.

CURBAR EDGE FROM NEW BRIDGE, PEAK DISTRICT © JOHN COEFIELD

EASEDALE TARN, LAKE DISTRICT © STEPHEN GOODWIN

AMBLE PIER © DAVID WILSON

01 Druridge Bay & River Coquet, Northumberland 20.9km/13 miles

A coast and country circular, taking in the beautiful beach of Druridge Bay and visiting the River Coquet settlements of Amble and Warkworth.

Druridge Bay Country Park » Druridge Bay » Hauxley Nature Reserve » Amble » Warkworth » St Oswald's Way » Togston » Druridge Bay Country Park

Start
Druridge Bay Country Park visitor centre car park (parking charge). GR: NZ 272998.

The Walk
The walk leaves a former opencast coal mine, now a country park, to join one of Northumberland's most popular beaches. Druridge Bay has amazing views along its 11-kilometre stretch, and its neighbouring nature reserves make it a wildlife haven.

The coal mining heritage of this area comes from rich coal deposits laid down millions of years ago, when the area was forest and swamp. Evidence of this geology is visible on rejoining the beach beyond Low Hauxley. Under dunes, but exposed on the sand by erosion, there's a black seam of fascinating fossilised forest.

The next port of call is Amble. A traditional and now modernised harbour village welcomes visitors in what is known

as the 'friendliest port in England', a reference to a 1930s telegram from RMS *Mauretania* as it passed.

Along the River Coquet, with views of its castle ahead, is the historic town of Warkworth. A town with many unique features, this is a significant place in Northumbrian history. From its rebel baron who secured the Magna Carta in 1215 (see St Lawrence Church), to the 13th-century burgage plots leading to the only remaining fortified bridge in England.

Warkworth's highlight, and sitting at the top of the village, is its 12th-century castle. A Percy family castle, this is one of North-umberland's finest unadulterated fortifications.

Leaving Warkworth, and briefly joining St Oswald's Way, the return leg goes through the village of Togston before returning to Druridge and the chance to enjoy the country park.

DRURIDGE BAY & RIVER COQUET

DISTANCE: 20.9KM/13 MILES » **TOTAL ASCENT**: 151M/495FT » **START GR**: NZ 272998 » **TIME**: ALLOW 6 HOURS
SATNAV: NE61 5BX » **MAP**: OS EXPLORER 325, MORPETH & BLYTH, AND 332, ALNWICK & AMBLE, 1:25,000
REFRESHMENTS: DRURIDGE BAY COUNTRY PARK CAFE; VARIOUS OPTIONS IN AMBLE AND WARKWORTH
NAVIGATION: STRAIGHTFORWARD » **BOOK**: *DAY WALKS IN NORTHUMBERLAND* BY DAVID WILSON.

01 Druridge Bay & River Coquet

Directions – Druridge Bay & River Coquet

➤ Leave the car park and follow signs for *Beach*, crossing the road and taking a path through trees to a wooden walkway. **Turn left** passing the World War II anti-tank blocks along the dunes. Follow the beach for 2.2km until you reach a sign on the left for *Togston Links car park*. **Leave the beach here.**

2 **Turn right and walk along the road**, which turns into a path. Pass a sign for *Hauxley Wildlife Discovery Centre 1km* and continue along the path. **Turn left** at a signed path junction towards the Discovery Centre. (If you don't want to visit continue straight ahead.) After visiting the Discovery Centre **retrace your steps** to the signed path junction and **turn left** (signed *Amble 3.5km*). After a short distance reach Low Hauxley, **walk all the way through houses** (following *England Coast Path* signs). Before the car park **turn right through dunes on to the beach,** where you can see the remains of a fossilised forest and views of Coquet Island. Continue along the beach. Before the end of the beach, **leave on the left via steps and a boardwalk,** through dunes to meet a track. **Bear right** along the track and pass a caravan park. Continue to follow *England Coast Path* signs to the rear of dunes and past a playground. The path leads on to Amble's South Jetty. Follow the jetty round to the harbour.

3 Walk through the modern harbour shops, and past the Northumberland Seafood Centre. **Turn right at the main road** and continue through the town centre via Queen Street. **Turn right on to North Street** – signed *Marina & Braid* – to meet a gravel track alongside the boat yard. The path then meets the River Coquet heading to Warkworth with views of Warkworth Castle ahead. Follow the path alongside the road all the way into Warkworth to meet a T-junction.

4 **Turn right at the junction** and walk along the road towards the castle. **Fork right** on to Castle Terrace; walk past the Sun Hotel then **take the small path to the right of Roxbro House** – signed *Warkworth Br ¼*. The path leads between burgage plots to reach the road and medieval bridge. **Follow the path to the left of the bridge** – signed *Monks Walk/Coast Path*. **Turn left after the church** to meet the main street. Stay on the right-hand side of the road heading for the castle.

5 Now on St Oswald's Way, **enter the castle grounds** at the top of the street and walk to the right-hand side of the castle. The path follows steps up to a car park and public toilets (open during castle opening hours). **Walk past the toilets on your right and follow the left-hand track to the main road**. Cross the road, **turn right then immediately left** – signed *Togston & Broomhill*. **Turn right on to Warkworth Avenue** (signed *St Oswald's Way*) and then **turn left on to a track**. Follow the track for 1.7km then at a signpost follow sign for *Togston 1,* leaving St Oswald's Way. After 750m and before the track goes through a gate, **turn left** on to a grass trail through trees. Keep straight ahead until you reach a hedge then **turn left** on to a path into Togston.

6 **Turn left at the main road**, pass a bus stop and **turn right on to Queen Street** to follow a path around the rear of gardens and allotments. As the track bears to the right follow it for 10m and then **enter a field straight ahead**. **Turn left** to follow the field border (with trees on your left) for four fields. At the corner of field/wooded area – signed *Public Footpath* – enter the trees (this path can be overgrown but is passable). Follow the path to copse edge, **turn right and look out for stile** to cross into the next field. On entering the field **turn right** and follow the treeline (on your right) all the way around to main road and take the track bending around to the subway.

7 Leave the subway and at road level turn right on to a track signed *Public Footpath*. The path leads to a Druridge Bay Country Park gate, **turn right** here and follow signs for *Lakeshore Walk*. After 450m **turn left down a track to a weir** and stepping stones. **Cross the stepping stones and turn left**. Follow the path along the lakeside all the way back to the start.

VIEW ALONG HADRIAN'S WALL © DAVID WILSON

02 Classic Hadrian's Wall Country, Northumberland

12.7km/7.9 miles

Walk in the footsteps of the Romans on this iconic circular route, following both Hadrian's Wall and the old Roman road, Stanegate. This is a true walk back in time.

The Sill » Stanegate » Vindolanda Roman Fort » Stanegate » Housesteads Roman Fort » Milecastle 37 » Sycamore Gap » The Sill

Start

The Sill: National Landscape Discovery Centre, Bardon Mill (parking charge). GR: NY 753669.

The Walk

This walk visits a popular section of Hadrian's Wall and features one of the country's most photographed trees at Sycamore Gap. In contrast to the well-walked sections along Hadrian's Wall, the route goes along one of the most important Roman roads in Britain, Stanegate – a quieter place to explore.

You begin your walk at The Sill: National Landscape Discovery Centre, built by Northumberland National Park as a gateway to the great outdoors. Take the time to explore the centre and find out about the local landscape and heritage, or visit afterwards for a bite to eat.

Leaving The Sill you will soon join Stanegate – look out for the milestone as you join the road. This road ran across the country and linked forts in Carlisle and Corbridge. Constructed 50 years before the Wall, it was a marching road with forts at one-day marching intervals (13 miles). One of these forts was Vindolanda, and is the first this walk visits. Leaving Stanegate you cross the Military Road – a road named for its military function during the 18th-century Jacobite rising. This road is also the main culprit as to why so much stone has now disappeared from the wall.

The next fort visited is Housesteads, one of the most complete forts in Britain. Now on the Hadrian's Wall Path, the walk heads west passing milecastle gateways as well as smaller turret installations. The route passes the internationally known Sycamore Gap, famed by the 1991 Kevin Costner film *Robin Hood: Prince of Thieves*. The final viewpoint before returning to The Sill is Peel Crags, where to the west you can see Winshield Crags, the highest point of Hadrian's Wall.

CLASSIC HADRIAN'S WALL COUNTRY

DISTANCE: 12.7KM/7.9 MILES » **TOTAL ASCENT**: 316M/1,037FT » **START GR**: NY 753669 » **TIME**: ALLOW 4.5 HOURS **SATNAV**: NE47 7AN » **MAP**: OS EXPLORER OL43, HADRIAN'S WALL, 1:25,000 » **REFRESHMENTS**: THE SILL OR TWICE BREWED INN, BARDON MILL » **NAVIGATION**: STRAIGHTFORWARD ALONG WAYMARKED TRAILS **BOOK**: *DAY WALKS IN NORTHUMBERLAND* BY DAVID WILSON.

© DAVID WILSON

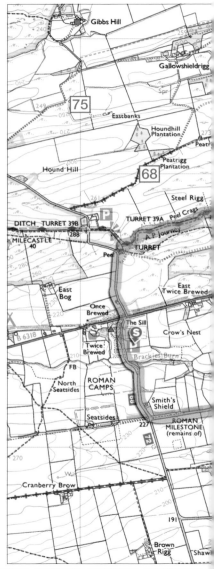

02 Classic Hadrian's Wall Country

Directions – Classic Hadrian's Wall Country

➤ From The Sill car park join the road and **turn right**. Follow the road past Smith's Shield House to a junction; **turn left** along Stanegate. Follow the road past a thatched house towards Vindolanda Roman Fort.

2 Before the fort, **turn right** following the sign for *Henshaw 1¼, Bardon Mill 2*. Go through a gate and follow the track to the next gate with a view of Vindolanda on your left. Go through the gate and follow the cobbled track down to road; **turn left** on the road towards High Fogrigg House. As you approach the house, **turn right on a permissive path** over a stile and take the **right-hand track**. At bottom of the track **turn left** to a gate. Go through the gate and walk to a stile on the other side of the field. Go over the stile, cross to the opposite fence line then **turn right to a further stile**. Cross into the next field and **follow the fence line on your right** all the way down to Low Fogrigg House.

3 **Turn left at the house** on to a track. Pass through two gates and continue to meet a wooden boardwalk. This leads to the bottom of the Vindolanda Roman Fort site and a bridge over a river. **Follow the signed path up to the right-hand side of the site** on to a road which leads offsite to the main road. At this point **drop left downhill** to visit the Roman Milestone (one Roman mile from the previous stone on Stanegate). **Retrace your steps back up to the road** and walk past the entrance and uphill to a T-junction. **Turn left and walk along the road.** Stay on the main road at the next junction, following *Newbrough 6*. This is the route of Stanegate. As you get to the top of the hill, with views of Grindon Lough ahead, arrive at a junction.

4 **Turn left along a bridleway** signed *Military Road*. Pass a farm and go through **two wooden gates to your right** on to a bridleway crossing a field – marked with ground posts. The track goes uphill with views of the Military Road and a stile ahead. Cross the stile then **turn right** and cross the road – **take care** as this is a fast road. **Join the road on your left** going through a gate signed *Housesteads ½*. Walk until you reach Housesteads Roman Fort.

5 **Walk between the visitor centre and the Roman Fort** to reach a gate and join the Hadrian's Wall Path National Trail. **Turn left** to walk the only section of Hadrian's Wall where you can go on top of the wall. From here follow the wall and pass Milecastle 37 before reaching the point where the Pennine Way meets Hadrian's Wall. Climb again going along Hotbank Crags with views across to Highshield Crags above Crag Lough. Drop down past Hotbank and briefly join the paved section of path. This leads **through two gates,** following the sign for *Steel Rigg 1½.*

6 Climb up through a copse of trees, over crags and reach Sycamore Gap and its famous tree. Beyond here climb again, drop down to Milecastle 39 and then along the wall to reach the top of steep steps down to a prominent section of wall and the remains of a turret. The Sill can be seen off to your left. Follow the path along the wall (on your left) and **take a gate on your left** and walk past Peel Cottage. **Turn left** and walk along the road, crossing the Military Road (B6318) to return to The Sill.

SYCAMORE GAP © DAVID WILSON

TAKING THE AIR ALONG LATRIGG'S CREST © STEPHEN GOODWIN

This short but scenic loop from Keswick takes you up Latrigg, Keswick's mini mountain, with a choice of routes back into the town.

Keswick » Cumbria Way » Mallen Dodd » Latrigg » Underskiddaw » Keswick

Start

Junction of Brundholme Road and Spooney Green Lane, Briar Rigg, Keswick. There are several pay and display car parks in Keswick. GR: NY 267241.

The Walk

Latrigg rises in Keswick's backyard, a modest 368 metres in height, but a perfect example of the old adage that 'good things come in small packages'.

Viewed from the town, Latrigg has an inviting profile: a partially wooded, fairly steep south-facing slope rising to a clean summit ridgeline. Though it appears from this angle a hill in its own right, Latrigg is in fact a southerly outlier of the Skiddaw massif.

An ascent of Latrigg is hardly a big day out. The round proposed here takes about two and a half hours at a regular pace. Of course deep snow would pro-long the walk, but that is rarely a factor on such a low hill. A more likely cause to be delayed along the bare crest is the perfection of the panorama it offers: south across Keswick, down the length of Derwent Water, then squeezing between the craggy jaws of Borrowdale to soar over the serried heights of Gable, Great End, Glaramara and all the central fells.

One of Latrigg's particular merits is that it offers a breath of air and exercise even when hostile weather has closed down the higher fells. The walk described here is straightforward; boots will be needed if there is snow (or it is wet); and even if the sun is shining, don't forget a wind-proof. Latrigg may be close to town but even when it's relatively calm in the centre of Keswick a keen wind can be gusting over the summit. Just look at those larches below the crest, shaped by prevailing south-westerlies into studies for sketchers and water-colourists, gems in this small package.

LATRIGG

DISTANCE: 6KM/3.7 MILES » **TOTAL ASCENT**: 310M/1,017FT » **START GR**: NY 267241 » **TIME**: ALLOW 2.5 HOURS
SATNAV: CA12 4NN » **MAP**: OS EXPLORER OL4: THE ENGLISH LAKES: NORTH-WESTERN AREA, 1:25,000
REFRESHMENTS: PHEASANT INN, CROSTHWAITE, AND NUMEROUS OPTIONS IN KESWICK » **NAVIGATION**:
STRAIGHTFORWARD » **BOOK**: *WINTER WALKS IN THE LAKE DISTRICT* BY STEPHEN GOODWIN.

Directions – Latrigg

➡ Follow Spooney Green Lane **north-east** over the A66 (bridge), past a cottage on your left and through a gate into the edge of woods. Continue on the main path uphill for 1.5km. By now a cut plantation is on your left and the open slope of Mallen Dodd and Latrigg on your right.

2 At a fingerpost sign to *Latrigg summit* **turn sharp right**. The path now climbs more steeply in long zigzags before rising steadily southwards to a viewpoint at the west end of Latrigg's summit crest. There is a bench here (usually occupied!). **Turn left** and follow the crest path (heading east-north-east) for 250m to the highest point, unblemished by any large cairn.

3 **Continue along the crest path** and go through a gate. The path drops more steeply here, then, about 300m after the gate, levels out somewhat.

4 Here you have a choice.* To continue on a loop to the north-west of Latrigg summit, bear off **left** at this levelling and descend the field northwards to an obvious track across the base of a field and above woods. **Turn left** on to the track and follow it north-west to a small car park at the head of Gale Road. (The car park is at the foot of a major path to Skiddaw.)

OR *For an alternative route: from point **4** do not bear off so steeply but continue down, still leftwards, to the same obvious track as in point **4**, but 100m or so further east, at a metal gate. Go through the gate and continue gently down, curving southwards to another gate, almost 1km from the first. Go through the gate and **turn right** on to a tarmac lane. Follow the lane through Brundholme Wood and on a bridge over the A66 to reach Brundholme Road – a distance of some 3km. **Turn right** on to Brundholme Road to reach the start point at Spooney Green Lane.

5 Cross the car park to its north-west corner and go through a gate on to a path signed *Public Bridleway to Keswick*. Follow this past point **2** and continue down on the outward route to the start point on Spooney Green Lane.

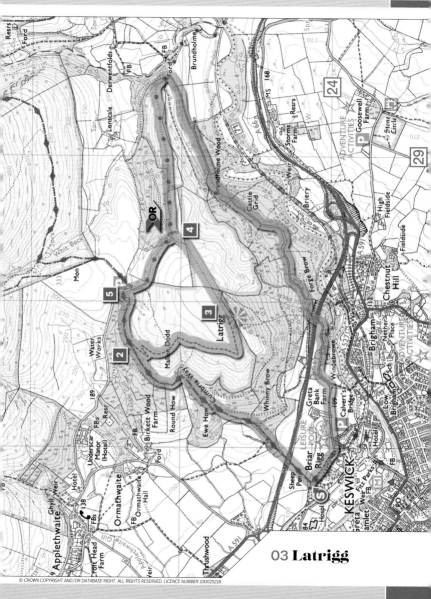

03 Latrigg

HEADING FOR LINGMOOR, CHAPEL STILE BELOW © STEPHEN GOODWIN

A Langdale round of mines, moor top and meadow.

Elterwater » Banks Quarry » Lingmoor Fell » Brown How » Side Pike » upper Great Langdale » Chapel Stile » Elterwater

Start

The Britannia Inn, Elterwater. Parking either at Walthwaite Bottom (just north of the village) or Elterwater National Trust Car Park (both parking charge). GR: NY 328048.

The Walk

Ideally, this easy walk should be done in the bloom of late summer for the old name 'Lingmoor' translates as 'heather moor' and even in these over-grazed times it still holds true. The artist William Heaton Cooper thought it 'a good place on which to laze away a summer day in the heather, listening to the hard-working bees and the distant waters of the Langdales'.

We start out from Elterwater alongside Great Langdale Beck. On the opposite bank is the Langdale timeshare complex built on the site of the former Elterwater Gunpowder Works.

Gaining height, we pass through mixed woodland to the disused Banks Quarry and then on to the open fellside above Langdale. A feature of this walk is the changing view of the Langdale Pikes, really superb from Brown How, the rocky knobble that forms the summit of Lingmoor.

The undulating walk over Lingmoor ends at a col with the craggy east face of Side Pike directly ahead. We skirt this via a narrow path at the base of the rock, with an improbable squeeze by a detached pillar and gain Side Pike from the west.

Descending to Great Langdale, where the Hikers' Bar at the Old Dungeon Ghyll Hotel might be a tempting diversion, the return half of the walk is mainly over valley farmland. We pick up the Cumbria Way at Side House Farm and then follow this for the remaining five kilometres into Elterwater.

LINGMOOR FELL & SIDE PIKE

DISTANCE: 12KM/7.5 MILES » **TOTAL ASCENT**: 597M/1,959FT » **START GR**: NY 328048 » **TIME**: ALLOW 5 HOURS **SATNAV**: LA22 9HP » **MAPS**: OS EXPLORER OL6, THE ENGLISH LAKES: SOUTH-WESTERN AREA, AND OL7, THE ENGLISH LAKES: SOUTH-EASTERN AREA, 1:25,000 » **REFRESHMENTS**: THE BRITANNIA INN, ELTERWATER; WAINWRIGHTS' INN, CHAPEL STILE; HIKERS' BAR, OLD DUNGEON GHYLL HOTEL » **NAVIGATION**: TAKE CARE THROUGH THE SLATE WORKINGS AT CHAPEL STILE, WELL SIGNED BUT A WORKING SITE » **BOOK**: *DAY WALKS IN THE LAKE DISTRICT* BY STEPHEN GOODWIN.

Directions – Lingmoor Fell & Side Pike

➲ From The Britannia Inn in Elterwater, cross Great Langdale Beck on a road bridge. **Turn right** (upstream) on the riverside path.

2 After almost 1km, after passing (but **not crossing**) the footbridge at rear of Wainwrights' Inn, Chapel Stile, the **path swings left**, away from the river, up to quarry workings, passing through a short 'cutting' of stone walls.

3 **Turn right** on reaching a tarmac lane and follow *footpath* signs through the site, with the slate cutting sheds on your right. Exit works by site office and into woods. At a junction with a track (cottage on your right), **turn right and immediately left** up a path signed *PF Little Langdale*. After about 50m, **turn right** on a former quarry track. The track ascends gently, passing the disused Banks Quarry.

4 600m after Banks quarry, **turn sharp left** on to a path that zigzags up the fellside; the path is marked by a small cairn and arrow roundel on a short stake. In about 10 minutes reach a locked green iron gate with steps. Climb over and **turn right** up the slope to a cairn and onward on a grassy path between bracken.

5 **Turn right** at a T-junction with the path coming up from Little Langdale on your left. The path ascends with a ridge wall on your right to a viewpoint with slate bench/windbreak and cairn. Continue around a spoil heap and along the undulating fell top. After a small tarn near a bend in wall, the path ascends Brown How, the highest point on Lingmoor Fell. Cross a stile over a wire fence to summit the cairn (469m).

6 Continue on the path heading north-west, at first by a fence, but the fence soon swings away. Cross a knobbly outcrop then go steeply down by a wallside and over a stile. Continue down to a col.

7 At the col*, with Side Pike ahead, cross a stile, ascend to the foot of the crag and follow the path **leftwards** below the crag, at one point squeezing between the crag and a detached pillar. **Take care**, the path is briefly exposed on left. The path ascends rightwards on to Side Pike. On the ridge, **fork right** to visit the summit (362m), then return to this point and descend the worn path westwards, with occasional small rocky steps to reach the road at a cattle grid.

04 Lingmoor Fell & Side Pike

OR *To miss out the 'squeeze' path and Side Pike, **turn left** at **7** and descend directly to the road. **Turn right** and follow the road to reach the cattle grid at **8**.

8 **Turn right** along the road then continue **straight ahead** on an engineered path to descend northwards into Great Langdale towards woods near a campsite (Old Dungeon Ghyll Hotel beyond). A wall and road are on your left-hand side while descending. Shortly before reaching woodland **turn right** on a worn grassy path that dips after passing the wood end to join a more defined path heading east across fields towards Side House Farm.

9 Just above the farm, cross a ladder stile and footbridge, descend on the streamside (**do not** cross to farm) and continue eastwards across field. After a kissing gate veer up hillside, path cobbled, through an old sheepfold, then down. This is the (waymarked) Cumbria Way.

10 At the junction at Oak Howe (next to a barn and cottage), follow the signed path *PB Gt Langdale Road* heading past the cottage.

11 1km after Oak Howe, cross the river at New Bridge. Just before reaching the road, **turn right** on a track and follow this past Thrang Farm, Chapel Stile, and join the road shortly before Wainwright's Inn. Just beyond the pub, **turn right**, signed *PF*, and cross the footbridge to rejoin the outward route at **2**.

CROSSING LINGMOOR © STEPHEN GOODWIN

GOATHLAND STATION © TONY HARKER

An easy walk over moorland and pastures with waterfalls, steam trains and wonderful scenery.

Goathland » Mallyan Spout Hotel » West Beck » Hazel Head » Julian Park » Carr Wood » Beck Hole » Darnholm » Goathland

Start

Goathland car park (parking charge).
GR: NZ 833013.

The Walk

This short loop starting in Goathland packs a lot of varied walking into its 11 kilometres and, although there is almost 400 metres of ascent, the climbs are short. The alternative route to Thomason Foss is highly recommended, but it can be dangerous in parts and may not be ideal for the unsure footed. Enjoy fantastic scenery all around on this magnificent walk.

We start from the car park taking the road west towards The Mallyan Spout Hotel. From here we pick up a classic winding moors path contouring above Hunt House Road on the lower slopes of the moor. The path offers good views over towards Wheeldale Moor and the valley of Bumble Wood. After the moor the terrain turns to pasture as we cross West Beck before the biggest climb of the day to Hazel Head Farm.

A short bit of road walking leads us to a wonderful path through Carr Wood. The path meanders through the trees dropping into the charming hamlet of Beck Hole and an opportunity for refreshment at the famous Birch Hall Inn. If you are in a group larger than six there won't be much room for you in the bar! From Beck Hole the more adventurous can enjoy the rough track towards Thomason Foss waterfall. The more sheepish will climb to the safer moors path. Both routes lead us on to the beautiful ford area at Darnholm before we finish above Goathland Station (watch for the steam train!) taking the road back to the start.

GOATHLAND & HAZEL HEAD

DISTANCE: 11KM/6.8 MILES » **TOTAL ASCENT**: 360M/1,181FT » **TIME**: ALLOW 3 HOURS **SATNAV**: YO22 5LX » **MAP**: OS EXPLORER OL27, NORTH YORK MOORS: EASTERN AREA, 1:25,000 » **REFRESHMENTS**: THE GOATHLAND HOTEL, THE MALLYAN SPOUT HOTEL, THE INN ON THE MOOR HOTEL, GOATHLAND TEA ROOMS, THE MOORS COFFEE SHOP – ALL GOATHLAND; BIRCH HALL INN, BECK HOLE » **NAVIGATION**: MOSTLY WELL SIGNED, BUT FREQUENT REFERENCE TO MAP IS RECOMMENDED ESPECIALLY OVER THE MOORLAND SECTION » **BOOK**: *DAY WALKS IN THE NORTH YORK MOORS* BY TONY HARKER.

© TONY HARKER

05 Goathland & Hazel Head

Directions – Goathland & Hazel Head

➔ From the main car park **turn right** to reach the main road and then **turn right again**. Follow the road for 1km to the road junction at the Mallyan Spout Hotel. **Turn right** at the junction and then after just 10m **turn left** on to a grassy track signed *Public Bridleway*.

2 Follow this track contouring above Hunt House Road. The track becomes narrow and is a delightful walk around the moor with views opening up over Wheeldale Moor. After 1km the path forks: take the narrower **left fork** climbing the hillside towards a tall cairn.

3 At the cairn there is a small quarried area: **turn right** past the cairn on to a rock path following the edge of the escarpment and marked by cairns. **Bear right** after the last cairn in line, about 800m after the first one. The area is marked with a wide expanse of rocks. Follow the path down the hill strewn with rocks aiming for the left corner of the wood ahead.

4 **Turn right** briefly on the road for 180m and then **turn left** on to a wide track signposted *Roman Road* leading downhill through two gates to the concreted ford over West Beck. **Turn right immediately after the ford** before the metal gate following the bridleway arrow. This path leads up the hill to Hazel Head Farm.

5 Pass through the farm area through a double gate on to the lane. Follow this lane for 1.6km past Hollin House Farm to a sharp right-hand bend and road at Julian Park. **Turn left** and then after buildings **turn right** on to a footpath. Stay with this footpath through the field **ignoring** a left fork after 180m. The path turns left with the wall after another 480m and drops down to a stile leading into Carr Wood.

6 This is a delightful path through the woods. Follow it for 800m **turning right** at the signpost for Beck Hole. The path drops sharply down stone steps crossing a bridge* over West Beck again, through a gate on to the road at Beck Hole.

> **OR** *Or, at this point, just after the bridge, you have the option of the easier route back by **turning right** on to the Railway Walk track which takes you directly back to Goathland.

7   **Turn left** past the Birch Hall Inn and cross the bridge*. Continue along the road for 570m until you reach a path on the right just before a farm.

> **OR**   *Or, to take the more dramatic alternative, after the bridge **turn right** at the footpath and follow this up alongside a sharp edge eventually dropping alongside the stream. After 350m **turn left** up an earthy climb through the trees to a fence and railway. (Keep **straight ahead** with stream to view waterfalls and return). **Turn right** at fence and follow under bridge climbing to bench and wall corner. **Turn right** at path (rejoining the main walk at point **9**).

8   **Turn right** on to the footpath. Follow it for 400m to a wall corner and **turn right**. Drop downhill for 90m and **turn left** at the footpath sign. This path leads to another wall corner with a bench after 400m.

9   **Avoid** going straight ahead dropping to the valley but instead take the grassy path to the **left** gently climbing the contours to Lins Farm. Pass the farm and after the double gate **turn sharp right** down through the bracken and steps, over the bridge and on to a wide gravel track.

10   **Turn right** at the track towards the ford. Don't cross the ford but **turn left** just before the ford over the field. The path leads to steps climbing the side of the steep valley. Follow this path over the top above the railway, eventually dropping down to the station gate to the **right**. Cross the railway and continue straight up on to the main Goathland road **turning right** to return to the car park.

HARDRAW FORCE © BERNARD NEWMAN

An easy walk taking in the spectacular waterfall of Hardraw Force and an airy ridge walk with a fine prospect of Wensleydale.

Hawes » Hardraw » Hardraw Force » High Shaw » Pike Slack » High Clint » North Rakes Hill » Sedbusk » Hawes

Start

Penn Lane (A684), Hawes. Various parking options available in Hawes, including Gayle Lane car park (parking charge). GR: SD 875898.

The Walk

Wensleydale is far and away the prettiest of the Yorkshire Dales: a broad sweep of water meadows beside the Ure, rimmed with limestone scars, heading almost due east from its head in the Howgills to Bedale in the Vale of York. Queen of Wensleydale is the beautiful small town of Hawes, a honeypot of a place if ever there was one, but hugely attractive despite this.

From the village, a very pleasant stroll across the river flats brings you to the Pennine Way and a luxury paved footpath to the village of Hardraw. A visit to the falls is essential, a mini-Niagara thundering over a precipice of hard sandstone into a charming, well-kept valley of green lawns and picnic spots. Entry and exit to Hardrow

Force is from the Heritage Centre next to The Green Dragon Inn. There is an admission charge to visit the falls.

Having gained the fell road, which leads over to upper Swaledale, we soon reach a viewpoint and bench at High Abbotside. The views down Wensleydale from here are as good as any in the Dales, but perhaps it's best to wait a bit to picnic, away from the road.

Follow the shooting track on to the moor and picnic in the wild, amid gritstone and limestone outcrops. Once on the escarpment we can contour its rim or, if the weather turns bad, stick to the track, whichever way leads to an obvious descent to Shutt Lane and the impossibly pretty village of Sedbusk. The footpath leads obviously across the fields to rejoin the outward road at the river. Now you must face the shops and cafes of Hawes ...

HARDRAW FORCE & ABBOTSIDE COMMON

DISTANCE: 10.5KM/6.5 MILES » **TOTAL ASCENT**: 304M/997FT » **START GR**: SD 875898 » **TIME**: ALLOW 5 HOURS
SATNAV: DL8 3QR » **MAP**: OS EXPLORER OL30, YORKSHIRE DALES: NORTHERN & CENTRAL AREAS, 1:25,000
REFRESHMENTS: PUBS, HOTELS AND CAFES IN HAWES; THE GREEN DRAGON INN, HARDRAW » **NAVIGATION**: STRAIGHTFORWARD; LOWER FIELDS A BIT MUDDY IN WINTER » **BOOK**: *DAY WALKS IN THE YORKSHIRE DALES* BY BERNARD NEWMAN.

Directions – Hardraw Force & Abbotside Common

➔ From Hawes head north out of town on Brunt Acres Road, past the caravan site on your right and crossing River Ure at Haylands Bridge. Shortly after leaving the river the road crests a low escarpment; **turn left** here to follow a footpath signed *Pennine Way Hardraw ¾ mile*. Follow the good footpath through fields and on a slabbed path for 1km to rejoin the road in Hardraw village at The Green Dragon Inn.

2 There is an admission charge to visit Hardraw Force (entry and exit is from the Heritage Centre next to The Green Dragon Inn). After visiting the waterfall retrace your steps back to the road and **turn left** and **left again** between cottages to follow a footpath north, up across fields past West House to reach the lane west of Simon-stone Farm.

3 **Turn left** and, after 50m, **cut left down a ginnel**, which brings you back to the stream above the waterfall. **Turn upstream** along the path to join a lane at the campsite at High Shaw.

4 **Turn right** up the lane for 100m to cottages and a footpath to Sowry. **Double back left** above the caravan site where pleasant open walking leads across fields and over gated stiles for 500m to reach the stream at a small wood. **Turn right** along the river-bank path, over a stile, then head up across the fields to reach the road at a barn.

5 **Turn left** steeply up the road to a quarry and viewpoint of the dale at High Abbotside. A few metres further on, after a cattle grid, a well-made track **heads right** (east) up on to the open fellside – take this. It's a good spot for lunch with great open views.

6 500m from the road at a *Public Bridleway* sign, **turn right** and follow the track south-east, or the edge of the escarpment. After 1.5km the track dips and kinks. Leave the grey track, **turn right** (south) downhill on a curving grass path steeply through fields to a gate. **Continue curving to the left** alongside a small wood, then steeply down to a gate at a walled track – Shutt Lane.

7 **Turn right** down to the village of Sedbusk. At the main street – Sedbusk Lane – **turn right** and, after 50m, **turn left** through the wall at the footpath for Haylands Bridge. Descend gently across fields and gated stiles, crossing another road, then down again over a very old cobbled bridge to rejoin the road back into Hawes.

06 **Hardraw Force & Abbotside Common**

GREAT COUM FROM UPPER DENTDALE © BERNARD NEWMAN

An excellent walk over a shapely fell with superb views over Morecambe Bay.

Dent » Flinter Gill Falls » Hazle Gill Combe » Crag Hill » Great Coum » Green Lane » Flinter Gill Falls » Dent

Start

Dent village car park (parking charge). GR: SD 704871.

The Walk

Great Coum is a superb mountain in miniature, sitting comfortably like a great armchair above the secluded and strangely remote village of Dent, right on the western limit of the Yorkshire Dales National Park. Great Coum and its twin peak Crag Hill can easily be reached from closer and higher mountain roads to the east and west, thus saving a climb, but this walk is a pleasing loop starting in Dent.

From the car park skirt the village green to find the track that climbs steeply beside Flinter Gill. Breaking out at the top brings wide-open spaces and a strategically placed bench where the path meets the contouring fell track linking Kingsdale with Barbondale. Heading west, we soon reach a mossy, walled lane which takes a southerly curve, ever-steepening to the summit ridge. A brief detour west leads to the summit of Crag Hill and famous views of More-cambe Bay.

The return trip to the top of Great Coum can be taken either side of the ridge wall depending on the prevailing wind. You're never far from geology in the Dales and here is no exception. As you reach the rim of the Great Combe of Great Coum, it's easy to imagine the huge basin filled with a shallow dome of dazzling white ice, riven with blue crevasses. In fact the combe held one of the last glaciers to melt from the English hills a mere 11,000 years or so ago. Once you get your eye in you can see that the final ridge down to the quarry looks just like the lateral moraines so common in the Alps.

After a last dose of geology at the quarry – limestone packed with fossils (crinoids) – you're soon back at the track and a most agreeable return trip to Dent.

GREAT COUM

DISTANCE: 11KM/6.8 MILES » **TOTAL ASCENT**: 553M/1,814FT » **START GR**: SD 704871 » **TIME**: ALLOW 3.5 HOURS
SATNAV: LA10 5QL » **MAP**: OS EXPLORER OL2, YORKSHIRE DALES: SOUTHERN & WESTERN AREAS, 1:25 000
REFRESHMENTS: CAFES AND PUBS IN DENT » **NAVIGATION**: STRAIGHTFORWARD, FOLLOWING TRACKS AND WALLS
APART FROM CONTOURING SECTION TO RIM OF THE COMBE OF GREAT COUM » **BOOK**: *DAY WALKS IN THE YORKSHIRE DALES* BY BERNARD NEWMAN.

Directions – Great Coum

➲ From the car park entrance, cross to the narrow street opposite, left of the Memorial Hall, and walk south, up past the village green to a footpath signed *Flinter Gill*. After passing cottages the lane becomes a stony track, which climbs steeply alongside the Flinter Gill. After 1km the track emerges from the woods, and shortly reaches a T-junction with Green Lane at a gate and bench. Pass through the gate and **turn right** (west) on to the contouring moor track, a signed bridleway to *Keldishaw 1.5 miles*. (The track to the left is our return route.) Continue through a second gate and **turn left** immediately through a third gate.

2 Follow the walled grassy track which climbs gently southwards, through another gate to where it ends at a sheep pen. With the wall to the right, climb straight up the steep hillside for 1.8km to the ridge. A more level 100m brings you to a wall and double stile.

3 **Turn right** and follow the wall for 300m to reach the summit trig point of Crag Hill (682m). Return to the stile and follow the north side of the wall (heading east) for 650m past a cairn and over a wall to the summit of Great Coum (687m). If visibility is good, continue east to the head of the combe and drop down rightwards on a broad ridge to gain a path on a more narrow ridge which leads to a limestone quarry. In misty conditions, stay with the main ridge wall for 300m or so as it drops steeply eastwards to a narrow terrace.

4 **Turn left** (heading north-north-east) to contour along the terrace for 200m to the rim of the combe and so down the narrow ridge path to the quarry. An old track leads out of the limestone quarry steeply down to a gate at a walled track, Green Lane.

5 **Turn left** and follow Green Lane as it contours for 3km back to the junction with the track back to Dent. **Turn right** here to return to Dent.

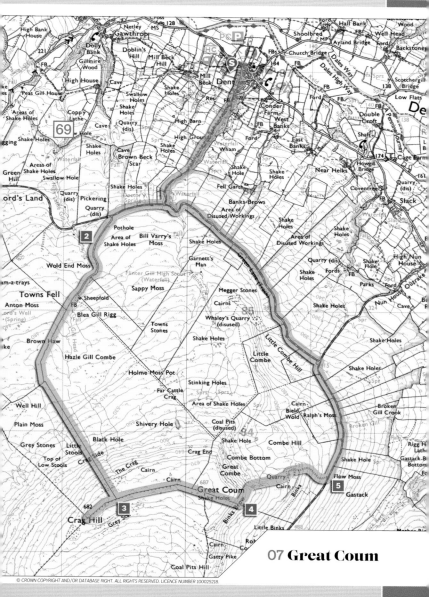

07 **Great Coum**

08 Hardcastle Crags, South Pennines

Walk this route in autumn when the leaf has fallen and covered the floor of Hebden Dale in the golden emblem of woodland.

New Bridge » Slack » Standing Stone Hill » Reaps Cross » Ridge Scout » Hardcastle Crags » New Bridge

Start

National Trust Midgehole car park (parking charge), New Bridge. GR: SD 988291.

The Walk

This is grouse shooting country and open access should be assessed before setting off on the walk. For the best experience walk this route in autumn to gain the full effect of golden leaves and earthy smells of the woodlands in Hebden Dale.

The walk starts from New Bridge at the bottom of Hebden Dale and ascends through beech and oak woodlands to small Pennine communities before heading out on to the moors. The first half of the route follows old ways across the Pennines, the stone marker at Reaps Cross denoting a medieval trail. The views across the moors and down the valleys are extensive and the ruined farmhouse at Raistrick Greave is very atmospheric. Perhaps this is due to the history of this part of Calderdale during the Civil War when a battle was fought around Heptonstall between the Royalists and Parliamentarian forces.

The walk down to Hebden Dale from Gorple Lower Reservoir follows Graining Water downstream as it cuts its way in to the gritstone rock. The footpath gives a high-level view of this narrow gorge and along the way the walker may come across boulder athletes honing their skills on the rock. Once past Black Dean the route begins to enter the woodlands that surround Hardcastle Crags. In autumn the ground and sky are filled with the golden hues of nature going to sleep before the coming winter, making for a pleasing experience. Hardcastle Crags can be easily missed off the forest trail so keep your eyes open for the path leading to them on the right. The view from the top of the crag along Hebden Dale is a good vantage point for birdwatching. Shortly after the trail passes Gibson Mill and a welcome break in the National Trust cafe before returning to New Bridge.

HARDCASTLE CRAGS

DISTANCE: 15.8KM/9.8 MILES » **TOTAL ASCENT**: 381M/1,250FT » **START GR**: SD 988291 » **TIME**: ALLOW 5 HOURS **SATNAV**: HX7 7AA » **MAP**: OS EXPLORER OL21, SOUTH PENNINES, 1:25,000 » **REFRESHMENTS**: WEAVING SHED CAFE, GIBSON MILL » **NAVIGATION**: GOOD NAVIGATION SKILLS REQUIRED » **BOOK**: DAY WALKS IN THE SOUTH PENNINES BY PAUL BESLEY.

WASHDAY ON THE MOOR AT POPPLES © PAUL BESLEY

08 Hardcastle Crags

Directions – Hardcastle Crags

➲ From Midgehole car park **turn left** and walk along the road and **turn right** to go across Hebden Water. On the opposite bank take the footpath to the **right** of a house up through woodland. Where the path intersects another go straight across and continue up, exiting via a flight of stone steps into open land.

2 **Turn right,** crossing a stile, and walk for **700m** then **turn left** along a walled lane to exit on to the road at Slack. **Turn right,** keeping **left** at the fork in the road and take the next footpath on the **left**. Follow the footpath across the area known as Popples to eventually cross the road on to a farm track. After 100m **turn left** and follow the farm track heading **west**, keeping **left** where it splits to arrive at a gate giving access on to the moor.

3 Follow the wall line **north-west** and at the corner of the wall maintain course across Black Mires passing the Standing Stone along the way to reach the Ordnance Survey triangulation pillar on Standing Stone Hill.

4 Go **west** across open moorland to Reaps Cross; continue in the same direction for a further **600m** then follow the footpath north-west across Heptonstall Moor to arrive at the abandoned farmhouse at Raistrick Greave.

5 Follow the footpath **north-west** through the ruins to reach the footpath running down the **eastern** side of Clegg Foot. Continue walking downstream and cross the footbridge over Reaps Water then ascend the opposite bank going over the stile on to the concrete track in front of the shooting cabin.

6 **Turn right** and follow the track downhill to Gorple Lower Reservoir. **Turn right** across the dam; **turn left** at the other end of the dam and **turn left** again to descend to the footbridge over Graining Water. Cross the bridge and **turn right** up the steep bank to reach Ridge Scout. Walk **east** past gritstone outcrops to reach a minor road.

7 **Turn right** to follow the road downhill; at the first bend **turn left** and go through a gate on to a wide track. After 70m **turn right** through a gate and down steps. Cross the footbridge across Alcomden Water and ascend the opposite bank. Walk along the waymarked footpath **east** across Black Dean eventually descending through fields to Over Wood.

8   Take the track along the front of the house and enter woodland. Follow the woodland trail for **1.4km** to Hardcastle Crags. **Turn right** to reach the top of the crag and enjoy the views. Retrace your steps back to the trail and **turn right** to reach the visitor centre at Gibson Mill.

9   From the visitor centre regain the trail and continue **south-east** through Hebden Dale to arrive back at Midgehole car park.

HARDCASTLE CRAGS © PAUL BESLEY

RIVER WYE WEIR AT CRESSBROOK © JOHN COEFIELD

09 Miller's Dale & Monsal Dale, Peak District
17.6km/10.9 miles

A combination of limestone upland and a deep, cliff-lined river gorge with plenty of industrial archaeology.

Miller's Dale » Blackwell » Priestcliffe » High Dale » Monsal Dale » Monsal Head » Cressbrook » Litton Mill » Miller's Dale

Start

Former railway station at Miller's Dale, just off the B6049. Parking at Miller's Dale car park (parking charge). GR: SK 138733.

The Walk

From the former railway station at Miller's Dale we follow the River Wye up Chee Dale for a short distance, before climbing out of the valley up a steep grassy hillside. Where this eases off, a close look at the terrain to the right of the path reveals hummocky ground that is the hut circle remains of an ancient settlement.

Continuing the climb through upland pastures our route leads to the hamlet of Blackwell. A mile of road walking along a quiet lane takes us through the scattered hamlet of Priestcliffe, from where an old walled track is followed above High Dale. This is forsaken for a woodland path that leads down to Monsal Dale.

The riverside path is followed to the footbridge and weir, before a climb leads to Monsal Head, where refreshments could be taken at either the cafe or pub. We then descend to the Monsal Viaduct and follow the Monsal Trail as far as Cressbrook.

After passing over the tumbling waters of the gorge below the millpond, we follow the riverside path through the limestone gorge of the beautifully named Water-cum-Jolly Dale to reach Litton Mill. Coot, moorhen, dabchicks and mallard are amongst the wildlife that babble around amongst the reeds along this section.

From Litton Mill there is a choice of routes. Either pick up the Monsal Trail and follow this back to Miller's Dale, or follow the more interesting quiet road alongside the river as far as the Anglers Rest before rejoining the Monsal Trail.

MILLER'S DALE & MONSAL DALE

DISTANCE: 17.6KM/10.9 MILES » **TOTAL ASCENT**: 600M/1,969FT » **START GR**: SK 138733 » **TIME**: ALLOW 5.5–6 HOURS **SATNAV**: SK17 8SN » **MAP**: OS EXPLORER OL24, THE PEAK DISTRICT: WHITE PEAK AREA, 1:25,000 » **REFRESHMENTS**: MONSAL HEAD HOTEL AND HOBB'S CAFE, MONSAL HEAD; ANGLERS REST, MILLER'S DALE » **NAVIGATION**: STRAIGHT-FORWARD ON WELL-USED PATHS AND TRACKS » **BOOK**: DAY WALKS IN PEAK DISTRICT: 20 NEW CIRCULAR ROUTES BY NORMAN TAYLOR & BARRY POPE.

09 Miller's Dale & Monsal Dale

Directions – Miller's Dale & Monsal Dale

➲ Walk to the front of the former station building and **turn right** on to the former railway track bed. Continue to the bridge before the viaduct and **turn right** to descend to the riverside path. **Turn right** and walk upstream to the footbridge – the first 200m require caution where the path slopes toward the river.

2 Cross the footbridge, **bear left** at first, then head up the steep grassy hillside taking the easiest line. The path straightens out as the slope relents. Cross a stile and keep a wall on the right. On reaching the start of a track, **follow this right, and then left** up to Blackwell Hall Farm. Stay on the farm drive, which leads to the road in Blackwell.

3 **Turn left** and continue down to a junction. Cross the main road and continue **straight ahead**. Pass through Priestcliffe Ditch and ascend to a road junction.

4 **Turn left** and follow the road to a hairpin bend. **Keep straight ahead** along a track for 100m, **fork right and then left almost immediately**. Follow the walled track for just under 3km to the cottages at Brushfield.

5 **Turn left**. Follow the track past the front of the cottages and through a gate. Continue on the high-level track for about 1km to level ground. There is a break in the track at this point and a path goes right down to Brushfield Hough Farm.

6 **Turn right** on this path, pass through the farm and then follow a track to a right-hand bend. Cross a stile in the wall **straight ahead** and continue down through woods to a junction with the path running through Monsal Dale.

7 **Turn left** to walk up Monsal Dale until you reach a footbridge.

8 Here you have two options*. To go via Monsal Head (for refreshments) and over the Monsal Viaduct **cross the footbridge** before the weir and ascend to Monsal Head. From Monsal Head, **turn left** downhill signed to the *Monsal Viaduct*; walk over the viaduct then continue straight ahead to reach a path junction.

🐟 *Or continue **straight ahead** following the river and pass under the viaduct. Carry on past a footbridge and ascend to the Monsal Trail at point **9**.

9   Follow the Monsal Trail but leave it for a **footpath on the right** before the tunnel which takes you down to a river crossing just below the millpond at Cressbrook. Cross the river then **turn left** and take the riverside path upstream below steep cliffs. Continue to Litton Mill.

10   At Litton Mill there is a choice of routes. To follow our recommended route, walk alongside the river on the quiet lane as far as the Anglers Rest, then cross the river at this point and ascend to the Monsal Trail, then **turn right** to return to Miller's Dale.

> **OR**   After passing through the former mill **turn left** opposite cottages to cross the river by a footbridge, ascend to the Monsal Trail then **turn right** to follow this back to Miller's Dale.

OLD MILL WORKINGS, CRESSBROOK © JOHN COEFIELD

CURBAR EDGE FROM BASLOW EDGE © JOHN COEFIELD

10 The Southern Gritstone Edges, Peak District

18.5km/11.5 miles

High-level footpaths, continuously changing views and impressive crags characterise this walk along the southern gritstone edges.

Baslow » Baslow Edge » Curbar Edge » Froggatt Edge » The Grouse Inn » White Edge » Gardom's Edge » Chatsworth Edge » Baslow

Start
Nether End car park, Baslow (parking charge). GR: SK 258721.

The Walk
From Baslow, a track leads us uphill to Wellington's Monument on Baslow Edge. The gritstone edges form an escarpment, two-tiered for some of its length. From these abrupt crags, so popular with climbers, the slope descends gently eastwards.

On its outward journey, our route follows paths north along the top of Baslow, Curbar and Froggatt edges, then climbs slightly higher to the overlying escarpment of White Edge. The path along here leads us south, then continues along the top of the much less frequented Gardom's Edge.

We also take in Chatsworth Edge, before finally descending through Chatsworth Park to finish.

The views along the way justify the popularity of these cragtop footpaths, although some sections along White Edge can be muddy after wet weather. A short exposed section of footpath along the top of Chatsworth Edge can be a problem for those that suffer from vertigo, but this can be avoided by taking a lower-level footpath.

Deer can often be sighted in Chatsworth Park – an added bonus on this route.

THE SOUTHERN GRITSTONE EDGES

DISTANCE: 18.5KM/11.5 MILES » **TOTAL ASCENT**: 500M/1,640FT » **START GR**: SK 258721 » **TIME**: ALLOW 6 HOURS **SATNAV**: DE45 1SR » **MAP**: OS EXPLORER OL24, THE PEAK DISTRICT: WHITE PEAK AREA, 1:25000 » **REFRESHMENTS**: THE GROUSE INN (POINT **4**) AND THE ROBIN HOOD (POINT **7**) » **NAVIGATION**: STRAIGHTFORWARD ON WELL-USED PATHS **BOOK**: *DAY WALKS IN THE PEAK DISTRICT: 20 CLASSIC CIRCULAR ROUTES* BY NORMAN TAYLOR & BARRY POPE.

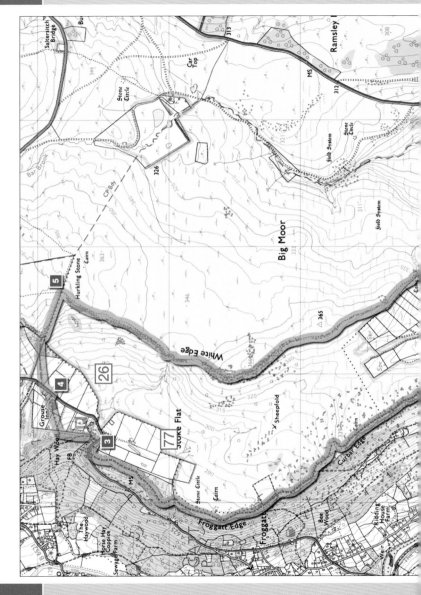

10 The Southern Gritstone Edges

Directions – The Southern Gritstone Edges

⮕ Cross the main road at the pelican lights and **bear left** up Eaton Hill. **Turn right** at School Lane and continue uphill along the road, then track, to Wellington's Monument.

2 **Retrace your steps** for a short distance then **bear right** and follow the broad path – or a narrower footpath along the top of Baslow Edge (optional route) – to the road at Curbar Gap. Cross the road, go through a gate and keep **straight on** along a broad path above Curbar Edge. The path continues above Froggatt Edge, eventually emerging at a main road.

3 **Turn right** and, in a short distance, go through a handgate over the road on the left. Descend to cross a stream and go up to Hay Wood car park. Keep **straight on** across and past the car park to reach a stile in the wall on the **right**. Cross it and continue across fields to rejoin the main road, just below The Grouse Inn.

4 Pass the inn, then cross the road to a gate. Go through the gate then follow the path up to a path junction. **Bear right** and follow the path with a wall on the right to a path junction.

5 **Turn right**. Follow the path along the top of White Edge for 3km. Shortly after the path begins to descend, the more well-used path descends steeply to the right. Instead, keep **straight on** along the less well-defined path to emerge near a road junction.

6 **Turn left**, continue to the road junction, then cross the main road and go through the gate on the **right**. **Bear right** to follow the path that runs more or less parallel to the road. Keep **straight on** through a handgate and continue in the same direction into the woodland above the crags of Gardom's Edge. Instead of following the often muddy and tortuous path by the wall on the left, make for the top of the crags, where the going is much easier and more pleasant with great views of the Derwent Valley below. Eventually you are forced back to the wall on the left, which leads down to a gateway. Once through this follow one of several options in the same general direction past Moorside Rocks and down to the main road.

7 Cross the main road to a stile almost opposite, then descend stone steps, cross a footbridge, and continue up to a track.* Cross this, continue over a ladder stile and follow the concessionary path along the top of Chatsworth Edge. A rail protects a short exposed section. The path descends a little after the crags peter out, crossing two stiles, then climbs again to resume its former course.

> **OR** *The path along the top of Chatsworth Edge is exposed over a short section. This can be avoided by **turning right** along the track to walk under the crags and enter Chatsworth Park at a lower level. Should this option be taken, on entering the park continue in the same general direction as the track just used.

8 After crossing a high stone stile, **turn right** and descend through Chatsworth Park, **bearing half left** away from the boundary wall on the right, initially using an old grassed-over quarry track. There are stiles across a wooden fence at regular intervals, to permit access to the tarmac drive. Cross this, aim for the left edge of a wood, and continue to a junction with a prominent footpath. **Turn right**, pass through a turnstile then continue into Baslow.

DEER BELOW WHITE EDGE © JOHN COEFIELD

Section 2

Southern England

Whether you want to find tranquility on the South Downs or explore the southernmost tip of England at Lizard Point, Southern England has some impressive and varied walking country. From the picture postcard villages of the Cotswolds to Bronze Age settlements on Dartmoor to the nature reserves and beaches of Norfolk, there is something for everyone here.

THE WRECK OF THE SHERATON BENEATH HUNSTANTON CLIFFS © ANNA PAXTON

Hunstanton Cliffs to Titchwell Marsh, East Anglia

11.3km/7 miles

A linear route following the Norfolk Coast Path from Hunstanton's dramatic crumbling cliffs, past a shipwreck, then through bird hides in the Holme Dunes and Titchwell Marsh nature reserves.

Hunstanton » Cliffs and Beach » Old Hunstanton » Holme next the Sea » Holme Dunes Nature Reserve » Thornham » Titchwell Marsh Nature Reserve » Coasthopper bus » Hunstanton

Start
Southend car park, Hunstanton (parking charge). GR: TF 672407.

The Walk
Our route takes us along a stunning stretch of the Norfolk Coast Path, with points of geological, historical and ecological interest. From the popular seaside town of Hunstanton, we explore the beach with its distinctive red-and-white striped cliffs. As rugged cliffs give way to reedbeds, saltmarsh and freshwater lagoons, we continue on to reach our destination at RSPB Titchwell Marsh. A short bus ride returns us to Hunstanton.

The cliffs of Hunstanton were formed by an unusual combination of iron-stained sandstone and chalk. Be aware that the sea comes in all the way to the cliffs at high tide, so check before leaving that the tide will be out (there is an alternative route on top of the cliffs if the tide is in).

Allow time to explore rock pools on the beach and search for fossils ejected from the chalky layer of the cliff. The remains of the *Sheraton* can be found on the beach – the *Sheraton* was a trawler dating from the early 1900s that was used as a military target hulk and wrecked in 1947.

Our route continues through Holme Dunes, where there is a visitor centre, cafe and beach, as well as the separate Holme Bird Observatory where visitors can use the bird hides for a small fee.

We finish our walk at Titchwell Marsh, temporary home to thousands of migrating birds throughout the year. One of the RSPB's most popular reserves, there is a wide sandy beach, a cafe and a visitor centre to enjoy before returning to Hunstanton on the bus.

HUNSTANTON CLIFFS TO TITCHWELL MARSH

DISTANCE: 11.3KM/7 MILES » TOTAL ASCENT: 63M/207FT » START GR: TF 672407 » TIME: ALLOW 3 HOURS (PLUS EXTRA TO EXPLORE RSPB TITCHWELL MARSH) » SATNAV: PE36 5AR » MAP: OS EXPLORER 250, NORFOLK COAST WEST, 1:25,000 » REFRESHMENTS: THE ORANGE TREE INN, THORNHAM; RSPB TITCHWELL MARSH VISITOR CENTRE CAFE, TITCHWELL » NAVIGATION: STRAIGHTFORWARD » BOOK: *DAY WALKS IN EAST ANGLIA* BY ANNA PAXTON.

Directions – Hunstanton Cliffs to Titchwell Marsh

From Southend car park **turn right** while facing the seafront and leave the car park to walk along the esplanade, which leads to a green and amusement arcade. After the amusements, **bear left** and continue along the North Promenade past Hunstanton Sailing Club. At the end of the promenade go down a set of stone steps which lead to the beach.

2 Continue **straight ahead*** along the beach with the red and white striped cliffs on the right. A white lighthouse and square red-brick watchtower will come into sight, after which the cliffs get smaller and give way to sand dunes. At this point, **bear right** towards the dunes, then **turn right** up a concrete ramp. At a well-hidden wooden post with an acorn symbol, **turn left** and follow a sandy track through overgrown trees.

OR *Or, if the tide is in, stay on the path above the cliffs which will rejoin this route at **3**.

11 Hunstanton Cliffs to Titchwell Marsh

3   Continue **straight on** past a series of wooden beach huts and the Ancient Mariner Inn. Continue along the footpath, following the *Norfolk Coast Path* signs past Hunstanton Lifeboat Station and Old Town Beach Cafe. Continue **straight on** along the footpath through the dunes, next to Hunstanton Golf Club. At this point it is possible to cut up to the left to join a parallel higher path which gives a view across the wetlands to the sea. The boundary of the golf course is marked *Private Property*; **bear right** and stick to the waymarked path which leads to an information board and multiple signposts. Continue **straight on** following the sign for the *Norfolk Coast Path* along a pebbly track which leads through the fens and into Holme Dunes Nature Reserve.

4   Follow the slightly raised path **straight ahead** through the nature reserve as it becomes a wooden boardwalk. Pass shingle bars and the site of Seahenge on the left, then approach woodlands directly ahead. Enter the woodlands along another wooden boardwalk, where there are signs indicating access to the beach on the left and Holme Dunes Visitor Centre (with a cafe and toilets) on the right. Take time to wander around the beach and visitor centre, then return to the signpost and continue **straight ahead** along the Norfolk Coast Path.

5   Continue along the path which leads up a wooden boardwalk to Holme Bird Observatory on the right. This is a separate reserve and there is a small charge to go in and use the bird hides. After the observatory, continue along the sandy track which bears right and then left, with very flat land on both sides of the raised path. At the waterway, **drop left** down an embankment and on to a narrow track, then **turn left** off the track, following signs for the *Norfolk Coast Path*. Cross a small wooden bridge then **turn right**, and **right again** on to a small road which leads into the village of Thornham. Walk past the church to reach a road junction next to a bus shelter and The Orange Tree pub.

6   **Turn left** and walk along the road for 1.5km to reach a signpost for RSPB Titchwell Marsh.

7   After exploring RSPB Titchwell Marsh, return to Hunstanton using the regular Coasthopper bus service. The bus stop is opposite the entrance to RSPB Titchwell Marsh and the journey takes around 25 minutes.

12 Owlpen & Hetty Pegler's Tump, Cotswolds   16.3km/10.1 miles

Sharp, steep hills, both up and down, with rewarding views, an outstanding Cotswold manor house and a long barrow to explore.

Uley Bury » Cam Long Down » Cam Peak » Downham Hill » Uley outskirts » Owlpen » Nympsfield » Hetty Pegler's Tump » Uley Bury

Start
Crawley Hill (B4066), Uley. Lay-by next to Uley Bury. GR: ST 787993.

The Walk
Follow the Cotswold Way down a steep track from Uley Bury and up, down and around Cam Long Down, Cam Peak and Downham Hill. These are small outcrops from the main limestone ridge of the Cotswolds, and were once surrounded by – if not under – water. Downham Hill was, much later, the site of an isolation hospital, hence the local name of Smallpox Hill. After crossing the valley the route passes close to Stouts Hill, a Gothic Revival house built in 1743 by the Gyde family of local mill owners. From 1935 to 1979 this was a school educating amongst others Stephen Fry and (Capt.) Mark Phillips, former husband of Anne, Princess Royal.

The hamlet of Owlpen is best known for its grade I listed Tudor manor house. After 80 years of neglect, it was saved in 1926 with careful Arts and Crafts style repairs.

The house and gardens are now open for pre-booked tours, or hired out for weddings, and there are several holiday cottages available for rent. It is worth a very short detour to visit the Church of the Holy Cross: the stained glass is lovely, but less common are the mosaics and tiling in the chancel and tower.

At the northern end of the walk is the village of Nympsfield with its church and the Rose & Crown inn (dogs welcome in the bar) after which the route again joins the Cotswold Way. The intriguingly named Hetty Pegler's Tump can only be reached by a road out-and-back diversion, but this is one long barrow that the agile can crawl inside. Return to the start through undulating woodland on the Cotswold Way.

For those with too much energy, a stroll around the hill fort and SSSI that is Uley Bury offers another view of the Severn plain, and of some of the places visited on the walk.

OWLPEN & HETTY PEGLER'S TUMP

DISTANCE: 16.3KM/10.1 MILES » **TOTAL ASCENT**: 515M/1,690FT » **START GR**: ST 787993 » **TIME**: ALLOW 6 HOURS
SATNAV: GL11 5AN » **MAP**: OS EXPLORER 167, THORNBURY, DURSLEY & YATE, & 168, STROUD, TETBURY & MALMESBURY, 1:25,000 » **REFRESHMENTS**: ROSE & CROWN, NYMPSFIELD » **NAVIGATION**: STRAIGHTFORWARD
BOOK: *DAY WALKS IN THE COTSWOLDS* BY JUDY MILLS.

WEST FROM COALEY PEAK © ADAM LONG

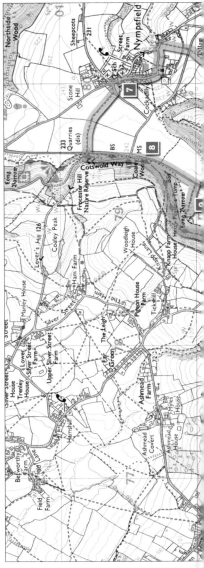

12 Owlpen & Hetty Pegler's Tump

➤ From the lay-by, take the **left** track (Cotswold Way) steeply downhill, following round left after it passes through Hodgecombe Farm and flattens out. **Turn right** at the road; the hill you are about to climb is ahead, so at a right-hand bend in the road go over a stile on the **left** and **straight up** on to Cam Long Down. Continue climbing through trees after a stile and at the top continue to the highest ground on your right with views over the River Severn and beyond. Follow the ridge along then follow the track down to a fingerpost, walking **ahead** signed *Cam Peak*. Climb up and down the other side, turning **left** on to a path before reaching the garden hedge (and **ignoring** 'ahead' arrow). There are several paths, all go roughly the right way but it is best to work your way down until the fence is close to your right-hand side. Go round the edge of Cam Peak then **right** through a kissing gate, and down the field to the road.

2 **Go straight across** on to a bridleway which is parallel to a drive. This may be very muddy (the tarmac drive with cattle grids may be easier walking). Stay on tarmac after the cattle grids and go through a gate on the **left** and between barns and through a yard. At the other side go **left** over a stile and cross the field diagonally toward barns, leaving the field over another stile and on to a track. Follow the track round the bottom of Downham Hill to a junction. Keep on the main track bending first right then keeping downhill to meet the road.

3 **Go straight across** on to the driveway of Sheephouse Farm. Go **straight ahead** to the end then follow arrow **right**, over a stile, bearing round **sharp left** on to a track. Before the stables walk **half right** to the top corner of the field (around a pond) and cross the stile. **Turn left** and go **straight ahead** to meet a track and road. **Turn right** at a *Restricted Byway* sign and stile leading steeply up into woods. At the path junction, go **hard left** and stay on the path close to edge of wood for just under 1km looking for a stile **left** leaving the wood (just before meeting wide tracks left and right). Walk down and **right** in field, aim for a double stile where there is a view across to Stouts Hill.

4 Follow the left-hand hedge to a corner then go **straight ahead** in a field to large, lone oak tree from where you will see a kissing gate ahead. Now go **half left** between trees to a stile in the bottom fence then go **half right** aiming to the left of Lye Farmhouse.

Follow the driveway to the road and **turn right**. Opposite a postbox **turn left** over a stile into a field. **Continue ahead** to stiles into second then third fields, look for (and use) a stile into a field on the **left** but continue on same line. Cross 4 stiles in quick succession then go **half right** to a stile in the field corner. **Continue ahead** and up to the next stile then **turn left** along the lower hedge to the road. **Turn right**.

5   **Walk uphill** to a sharp right-hand bend, entering a field on the **left** at a *Public Footpath* sign. Go diagonally downhill, then around to the **left** into the next field. Aiming to the left of the church, locate stiles to reach the bottom corner of field, and through young trees to the road. **Turn right** and continue around a left-hand bend. To visit the church **turn hard right** signed *Owlpen Manor*.

6   Return to the road and **turn right**. Continue until the road curves to the left; here go **straight ahead** on to a track signed *Owlpen Wood*. After around 1km the track bends sharp right. Leave the track on the **left** on or after the bend (exactly where depends on temporary fencing and mud!) to continue along the valley bottom with woods on both sides, before following a gentle curve **left** to a stile at the edge of wood. Go steeply uphill through the woods; leave the woods over a stile then cross via gateway/broken stile (maybe it is now mended) into a field on the right. Keep fairly close to the hedge on the left to reach a stile by the gate. **Cross the road** on to a short track opposite, then **continue ahead** over a stone stile and down into Nympsfield. **Turn left** at the road and **left** again to pass the church and the Rose & Crown.

7   Continue ahead then **turn left**; after a house **turn right** on to a track then into a field. Go over a stile and continue to a road. **Cross with care** and take the footpath **right** then **left**, (now on the Cotswold Way) to Coaley Peak. Continue through damp woodland to a road. Again cross, going uphill and round to the right.

8   Stay on the road, passing a *Cotswold Way* sign (you will return this way). **Continue with care** on the roadside for about 450m. **Turn right** to reach Hetty Pegler's Tump.

9   After exploring the barrow, backtrack to point **8** and **turn left** on to the Cotswold Way, following the undulating path through woods to the start.

THE CLIMB UP BLACKHORSE HILL © DEIRDRE HUSTON

13 Battle & its Wider Landscape, High Weald

13.8km/8.6 miles

This atmospheric route explores the undulating landscape around Battle Abbey and the renowned 1066 battlefields, taking in two very different woodlands and an ancient churchyard.

Battle Abbey » Great Wood » Blackhorse Hill » Crowhurst » Fore Wood Nature Reserve » 1066 Country Walk Bexhill Link » Battle Abbey

Start
1066 Battle of Hastings, Abbey & Battlefield car park (parking charge).
GR: TQ 747157.

Alternative start
Crowhurst Station (point 10)
GR: TQ 760129.

The Walk
Picnics are recommended for this walk, but another option is to walk early then enjoy lunch in Battle before exploring the abbey. The story goes that William the Conqueror founded Battle Abbey on the site of the Battle of Hastings as penance for the bloodshed, and our walk tries to give you a sense of the battlefield's location in the wider landscape. Contemporary sources, such as the Bayeux Tapestry and the chronicler William of Poitiers, inform our understanding of the Battle of Hastings. Harold's forces lined the ridge while the Normans were south on the other side of the marshy valley.

As you walk, think of the thousands of soldiers who fought a momentous battle on these Sussex slopes.

The pavement stretch at the start enables us to leave the town through Great Wood, a vast coniferous woodland. Our path is straightforward but could be muddy in winter. Before long, we climb Blackhorse Hill on what is possibly an ancient sunken path, formed by early farmers droving their pigs.

Later, nip into St George's churchyard to see the Crowhurst yew. The Ancient Yew Group estimates that the tree was probably planted on this sacred site by the South Saxons.

These days, Fore Wood Nature Reserve is so peaceful you might hear leaves whisper or an acorn drop. Ferns thrive in the shade of small steep-sided ravines in the sandstone: a typical High Weald gill.

BATTLE & ITS WIDER LANDSCAPE

DISTANCE: 13.8KM/8.6 MILES » **TOTAL ASCENT**: 280M/919FT » **START GR**: TQ 747157 » **TIME**: ALLOW 4 HOURS **SATNAV**: TN33 0AD » **MAP**: OS EXPLORER 124, HASTINGS & BEXHILL, 1:25,000 » **REFRESHMENTS**: VARIOUS IN BATTLE; THE PLOUGH INN, CROWHURST » **NAVIGATION**: STRAIGHTFORWARD THANKS TO WELL-SIGNED SECTIONS OF THE 1066 COUNTRY WALK BEXHILL LINK » **BOOK**: *DAY WALKS ON THE HIGH WEALD* BY DEIRDRE HUSTON.

© DEIRDRE HUSTON

13 Battle & its Wider Landscape

Directions – Battle & its Wider Landscape

➲ Exit the car park on the footpath. Pass a 1066 Country Walk (1066 CW) signpost and walk towards *Rye*. **Turn right** past the abbey entrance. Follow the path that runs beneath the wall. Pass St Mary's church on the opposite roadside.

2 Cross the road at The Chequers. **Walk left** at the roundabout, continuing **straight ahead** along Marley Lane following the signed 1066 CW. Walk down the hill and cross the railway line at the crossing. Continue on. Cross a minor road and then, when the pavement ends, cross the road to walk on the other side. Cross Harrier Lane and walk along the verge. Pass Blackfriars Oast.

3 Beside the gate to Greatwood Cottage, **turn right** along the signed bridleway and follow the 1066 CW through Great Wood. Pass a signpost and continue **straight ahead** past two waymarked crossroads. At the bottom of a hill, cross a stony track and pass a bench.

4 After 50m, **turn right** along the signed 1066 CW which you will see just after a *Sedlescombe* marker post. Walk up this steepish track. **Keep right** at the next signpost, staying on the 1066 CW. Emerge on a golf course and **walk right** for a few metres. **Turn left** on to the track and bridleway at a 1066 CW marker stump and walk through the golf course. Look out for a waymarker stump: walk **straight ahead** on the bridleway towards the side of a hedge. Walk on through the opening along the fenced path.

5 **Turn right** at the signpost to walk along a bridleway, leaving the 1066 CW. Go through a waymarked opening in a fence corner and walk **straight ahead** down the side of the grassy fairway. Keep going until you reach the bottom where, without crossing the ditch, you continue **straight ahead**, crossing the woodchip track, to where the bridleway enters some woods.

6 Go through a gate and **walk right** up the large field along the unsigned bridleway. At the top, **go left** through the **second** metal gate (note bridleway arrow on other side of the post) and continue on the fenced track. After a bit of a climb, pass a post where you join a rough driveway. Continue **straight ahead** on this bridleway/driveway. Pass a modern oast house/circular building. Views to the right make you realise how high you've climbed; there's more to come …

7 At the road, **turn right** to walk along the grass verge. Cross to use the pavement. Pass a red-brick chapel.

8 **Turn left** along Telham Lane. **Turn left again** along the track to Brakes Coppice Farm and Crowhurst Park Cricket Club. Walk along this unsigned public footpath. This is easy walking with far-reaching views.

9 **Turn right** through the waymarked walkers' gate along the signed footpath in front of the private farmhouse. At the end of the fenced path, go through a gate, cross a drive (there's a handy bench here for a rest stop) and descend the signed footpath down some makeshift steps. At the bottom, follow the signed footpath **left** to join the tarmac track. The footpath soon crosses the drive to Brakes Coppice Park (camping) and then joins it higher up as you head over the plank bridge and **straight ahead** up the hill. Walk along this pleasant tree-lined drive and through a white gate.

10 **Turn left** along the lane. Pass Crowhurst Christian Healing Centre. **Turn left** along the footpath to Crowhurst Station. Cross over the railway bridge and walk **straight on** into the village. Walk down this quiet street which boasts an interesting mix of old and new homes.

11 At Forewood Lane, **turn right*** (or nip into St George's churchyard to see the Crowhurst yew). Pass the school and the church as you follow the road round.

> **OR** *To divert approx. 500m to The Plough Inn at Crowhurst, **turn left** along Forewood Lane and then **turn left** along Chapel Hill. Retrace your steps to return.

12   **Turn left** round the gate at the waymarker signpost. This path leads to Fore Wood Nature Reserve and then Battle on the 1066 CW Bexhill Link. Walk straight up the edge and then across the middle of the field on the footpath. Walk along a mud track which descends through woodland. Go through a gate, noting direction of arrow. Head **slightly diagonally right** across the field on the footpath. Cross the stile and enter Fore Wood Nature Reserve. Follow the main path through the woods. Keep **straight on** at the marker post where the footpaths fork. The path climbs past a possible timber storage area. Walk on along this main track, **ignoring offshoots**. Pass a 1066 CW marker stump and descend past another marker post to exit through a kissing gate.

13   Cross a footbridge and walk **straight ahead** along the fence. At the signpost, **walk right** and pass a gate.

14   **Turn right** along the signed bridleway and road at the path junction in front of Powdermill Cottage. Walk down the hill. Cross a bridge over a stream and cover some ground on this easy walking lane. Pass The Old Coach House and Peppering Eye Farm. Continue **straight ahead** on this lane.

15   **Walk left** at the road junction, continuing on the signed 1066 CW Bexhill Link. **Take care** on this short stretch of road. At the next junction, walk **straight ahead** from the traffic island to cross busy Powdermill Lane and pass a walkers' post signing mileage to Battle. Climb over a stile and walk along the fenced footpath which runs above the road. At the top, go through a gate. Cross a lane and carry on **straight ahead** through a metal gate following the 1066 CW Bexhill Link. Notice Battle ahead of you on the ridge. Pass a couple of marker posts. Soon, a fenced path climbs gradually towards the battlefield. Go through a couple of gates and continue to climb along the side of grazing fields. Pass a signpost and walk **straight ahead** on a mud track. There's a pretty stream to your left but was this field such an idyllic site when the battle raged? Although it is hard to be certain how nearby that might have been. Keep **straight ahead** at the marker post. Go through a walkers' gate by a wall. Walk on towards the abbey and **either turn right** for the car park **or go straight on** to visit the battlefield site within the abbey or a local cafe.

FORE WOOD © DEIRDRE HUSTON

SWANBOROUGH HILL © DEIRDRE HUSTON

14 Vistas over Lewes Rape, South Downs

14.5km/9 miles

A sharp climb up to a downland ridge that offers extensive views from coast to castle, passing a top pub in Kingston before meandering through agricultural fields to Rodmell, home of Virginia Woolf, and a triumphant return along the River Ouse to peaceful Southease.

Southease » Mill Hill » Front Hill » Iford Hill » Swanborough Hill » Kingston near Lewes » Swanborough » Iford » Rodmell » River Ouse » Southease

Start

Roadside parking by Southease Church, accessible from lane off Kingston Road between Lewes and Newhaven. GR: TQ 423053.

The Walk

Pick up the South Downs Way in the peaceful hamlet of Southease. Southease Church is one of only three churches in Sussex to have a round tower. The 13th-century flint tower and wall paintings are significant, as perhaps once the village was: Southease is recorded in the Domesday book as having a thriving herring fishing industry.

This is a stunning stretch of the South Downs Way running along the ridge through rolling agricultural downland with ever-changing and exhilarating vistas over what was once the Norman 'rape' or district of Lewes. The views to the sea, over open fields, and on towards Sussex villages and Lewes town put life into perspective.

Descend to Swanborough or head on to Kingston with its 14th-century church and the much-loved Juggs pub. This friendly pub offers log fires, a cheerful terrace and garden, bustling atmosphere and good food.

Footpaths lead you on through crop fields, past barns and grazing horses. You never quite know when you're going to turn a corner and find a field of wild flowers basking in the reflected glory of the Downs.

The Abergavenny Arms in Rodmell is a traditional and welcoming pub with well-kept Harvey's beer and a frequently changing menu. Rodmell is also home to an 18th-century weather-boarded cottage called Monk's House. This was the country retreat of Virginia and Leonard Woolf. The National Trust house is open on certain days only (check online for details) when the local pub may fortuitously be offering cream teas.

VISTAS OVER LEWES RAPE

DISTANCE: 14.5KM/9 MILES » **TOTAL ASCENT**: 282M/925FT » **START GR**: TQ 423053 » **TIME**: ALLOW 4.5 HOURS
SATNAV: BN7 3HX » **MAP**: OS EXPLORER OL11, BRIGHTON & HOVE, 1:25,000 » **REFRESHMENTS**: THE JUGGS, KINGSTON, OR THE ABERGAVENNY ARMS, RODMELL » **NAVIGATION**: CARE NEEDED IN IFORD TO SPOT STILE AT POINT 9
BOOK: *DAY WALKS ON THE SOUTH DOWNS* BY DEIRDRE HUSTON.

14 **Vistas over Lewes Rape**

Directions – Vistas over Lewes Rape

➡ Pick up the South Downs Way (SDW) to walk up the lane to the top of the hill, passing to the right of the church. At the main road, **go right** to follow the SDW along the roadside. **Cross the road** and Gorham's Lane opposite, to go through the gate. Follow the clearly marked SDW across the field and then on to a track and through a second gate. **Turn left** by the signpost of the fence to walk along the hard-surfaced track.

2 **Turn right**, before the farm buildings, to **follow the SDW**. **Go right** through a gate and climb up a hill, still following the SDW. Go through a gate, cross the lane and follow the narrow path straight ahead running alongside the fence. At the end, go through a gate and follow the SDW **straight ahead** through agricultural downland crossing a byway through more gates by a signpost. **Continue straight on**. Pass through a gate and continue **straight ahead** on a long concrete bridleway through crop fields. **Easy to miss:** at the top of the slope, near the signpost, where the concrete path turns sharp left, **follow the grassy SDW right**. Follow the path as it **curves left through a gate**, running along Swanborough Hill.

3 At the signpost, you have a choice:

  ➤ **Take the right fork**, sweeping down towards Swanborough along Dencher Road. Follow the bridleway through the gate and then at the bottom of the hill, follow the marker posts as the track veers **left**. **Walk right** at the junction with the bridleway in the trees. The path turns into a concrete lane, running between houses. It rejoins the main route just before point **8** as it passes the marker post and Swanborough Manor.

  To continue on our main route to Kingston (and pub!), follow the stony bridleway as it curves round to the left then **straight ahead**. (Fabulous vistas!) Walk along the flinty bridleway then across the field. Pass a signpost and go through a gate.

4 At the signpost, **turn right**, leaving the SDW to head down the hill into Kingston. **Take care**: the compacted chalk may be slippery.

5 At the bottom of the hill, **turn right past two low wooden bollards** down the tarmac track. Continue along Church Lane. **Keep straight ahead at the recreation ground** and walk past the tennis court. At the corner, **follow the tarmac path left**. Beside the flint church, **turn right along the tarmac path**. Go through the gate and **turn left along the lane**.

6 Pass The Juggs pub and reach the road junction. Cross the road to walk on the pavement and **turn right** towards Newhaven along Ashcombe Lane. Pass the school and some houses.

7 Just after the *20 mph zone* sign, see the marker post on the far side of the road. **Turn right**, crossing the road to follow the narrow, signed footpath. Go through a gate and walk on. Go through a further gate and **walk straight ahead** through the farm buildings. Once through the farm, **veer left** on the track. **Walk straight ahead** past Swanborough Manor.

8 At the road, cross and **go straight ahead through a gate**. Follow the not obvious footpath across the field. See Lewes Castle to your left. **Turn right** at the marker post and walk in a straight line to the wooden fenced opening. Go through the opening and follow the path straight ahead. In the corner of the field, to the right of the metal gate, there is a stile. Follow the path straight ahead. Go over a stile and **turn right** in order

KINGSTON CHURCH © DEIRDRE HUSTON

to continue straight ahead towards the lane. Cross the lane, go over the stile and walk beside the flint wall and hedge. Go through a gate, cross the drive to Iford Manor, and through another gate, **continuing straight ahead**. Go through a metal kissing gate.

9 Go left to follow the lane a very short distance to the corner of a wall. **Turn right through an open gate** by an easy-to-miss disused stile and then **turn left to keep walking in the same direction** on the footpath (passing a cottage on your left) and on through the crop field and then straight on through next field of crops. At the bridleway, take a few steps right.

10 At the road, **take care and turn left** to follow it for a good 5 minutes.

11 Just after you leave Northease, at the metal gates, beyond Whiteway House, look for a signpost and footpath and **head left** leaving the road. Pass by the post and **follow the footpath straight ahead** through what appears to be a large back garden. Pass beside the tennis courts, over the stone steps and **straight ahead**. Go through the 'pinch' gate and along the footpath to the lane.

12 You are now in Rodmell.

> **OR** **Go right** to find the Abergavenny Arms up the lane.

Go left to continue on the main route past Monk's House. Stay on the lane until you pass the car park. Continue straight ahead, passing a stream and following the bridleway. Go through a metal gate. Pass a post and walk for a while. See Mount Caburn ahead. Go through another couple of gates and continue on.

13 At the river, **walk right**, through the kissing gate to follow the footpath along the riverbank. Walk through the kissing gate and continue on. See Southease Church spire to your right. Go through the gate at Southease Bridge.

14 **Turn right** to return to Southease Church along the SDW.

WILD FLOWERS IN CROP FIELD NEAR IFORD © DEIRDRE HUSTON

15 Haytor, Hound Tor & Widecombe, Devon

19km/11.8 miles

Starting at one of Dartmoor's most iconic tors, visit Hound Tor's medieval houses, the Grimspound stone circles and the pretty village of Widecombe in the Moor.

Haytor Visitor Centre » Haytor Quarries » Smallacombe Rocks » Becka Bridge » Greator Rocks » Hound Tor » Jay's Grave » Grimspound » Hameldown Tor » Hameldown Beacon » Widecombe » Top Tor » Hemsworthy Gate » Saddle Tor » Haytor Rocks » Haytor Visitor Centre

Start
Haytor Visitor Centre car park (parking charge). GR: SX 765771.

The Walk
The great, granite knuckle of Haytor, rising from the summit of Haytor Down, is an iconic image of Dartmoor. The 360-degree views from the top (it's an easy scramble to the very top should you wish) take in the surrounding moorland to Hound Tor, the Teign Valley with Castle Drogo in the distance and across the valley to the sea at Torbay.

We begin our walk through the quarries where granite was extracted between 1820 and 1919. Until 1858 the rock was transported on the Haytor Granite Tramway to the Stover Canal and was used for buildings across the country, including the rebuilding of London Bridge.

From a high moorland ridge we descend to Becka Brook, crossing on a traditional granite clapper bridge. From here we climb back up to Hound Tor, passing Hound Tor Deserted Medieval Village. Hound Tor is said to be the inspiration for Sir Arthur Conan Doyle's *The Hound of the Baskervilles*.

Quiet country lanes lead us to Jay's Grave, a small roadside headstone. Legend has it that a local woman, falling upon misfortune, hanged herself at a nearby farm and was buried here in the 18th century. There are always fresh flowers upon the grave. Ascending once again on to the high moor we pass Grimspound, a Bronze Age settlement of 24 stone hut circles surrounded by a low stone wall. Continuing along the glorious Hameldown Ridge brings us to the village of Widecombe, from where a final climb takes us back over the moor to Haytor.

HAYTOR, HOUND TOR & WIDECOMBE

DISTANCE: 19KM/11.8 MILES » **TOTAL ASCENT**: 627M/2,057FT » **START GR**: SX 765771 » **TIME**: ALLOW 5.5 HOURS **SATNAV**: TQ13 9XS » **MAP**: OS EXPLORER OL28, DARTMOOR, 1:25,000 » **REFRESHMENTS**: ULLACOMBE FARM CAFE, BOVEY TRACEY; THE RUGGLESTONE INN, WIDECOMBE » **NAVIGATION**: MOSTLY CLEAR PATHS AND A SHORT SECTION OF ROAD WITH SOME SECTIONS OF OPEN MOOR; NAVIGATION ON THE OPEN MOOR SECTIONS CAN BE TRICKY IN LOW VISIBILITY **BOOK**: *DAY WALKS IN DEVON* BY JEN & SIM BENSON.

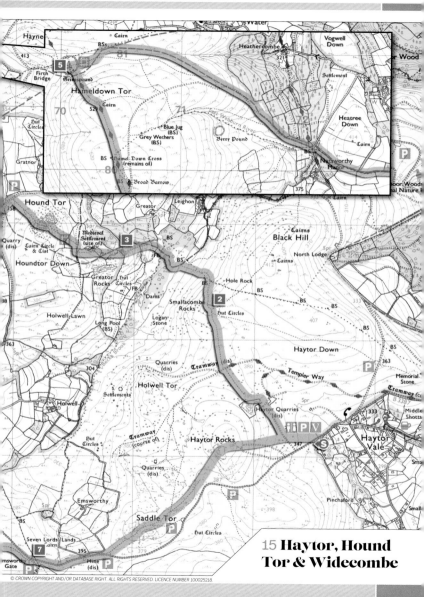

15 Haytor, Hound Tor & Widecombe

Directions – Haytor, Hound Tor & Widecombe

⮕ Cross the road and follow a wide path north-west towards the old piles of quarry stone. Pass to the right (east) of the quarry and join a section of the old granite tramway before taking one of the small paths on your **left** heading north. Cross another section of tramway and find the main path (probably **left** on the tramway for a short section) heading north to Smallacombe Rocks.

2 Find the path heading downhill from the north side of the rocks and follow it trending **left** to an open grassy area. Continue downhill into some woodland where the path gets very rocky. Cross the clapper bridge and head steeply uphill through three gates to emerge on to open moor at Greator Rocks.

3 **Continue downhill** initially and then up through a wall, past the medieval village and then up to Hound Tor. Pass between the rocks or to their left and head downhill to the road and car park. **Turn left** on to the road in front of the car park and then **turn right** at the road junction; follow this road for a little less than 1km to Jay's Grave.

4 **Turn left** and join the path behind the grave heading west over a hill to reach another lane. **Turn left** on the lane and then **almost immediately right** through a gate on to open moor. Follow the track across the stream and then uphill in a north-westerly direction. **Trend right** at the vague path junctions and cross the saddle to drop down slightly to Grimspound.

5 Take the path **left** uphill to the trig point and rocks on Hameldown Tor. Continue heading south along the ridge for about 3km, then take the path heading **left** and downhill, joining a lane and turning **right** into Widecombe.

6 Follow the road east through Widecombe with the church on your right, and continue following the B3387 uphill back on to the moor. Shortly before the top of the hill take a track heading **right** (south-east) from a parking area towards a pile of rocks and then up to Top Tor. Continue past the tor and head downhill to the road junction and cattle grid.

7 Cross the road and follow it east to the car park below Saddle Tor where the road bends to the right. Follow the path uphill here to Saddle Tor and then **continue ahead** towards Haytor. Follow the path around to the **left** of the huge wall of Low Man and continue around until you emerge in the avenue between the two rock exposures. Walk between the rocks and then trend **left** around Haytor and downhill back to the car park.

DARTMOOR PONY NEAR SMALLACOMBE ROCKS © JEN & SIM BENSON

16 Around Lizard Point, Cornwall

13.5km/8.4 miles

A walk around mainland Britain's most southerly point taking in the area's fascinating history, geology and wildlife.

Lizard village green » Church Cove » Bass Point » Housel Bay » Lizard Point » Kynance Cove » Lizard Downs » Lizard village green

Start

Lizard village car park, next to the village green. GR: SW 703125.

The Walk

The Lizard Peninsula is the most southerly part of Britain's mainland, a unique place with a distinct character, partly because of its separation from the main arm of Cornwall, but also because of its unusual geology. The metamorphic rocks on which the peninsula lies are dark green in colour, veined with red and white, named serpentinite for their resemblance to snakeskin. The relentless sea has carved the coastline into an intricate maze of coves and caves, perfect for exploration on foot or by boat – the sea kayaking is also outstanding here.

Our walk begins in Lizard village, a friendly community with plenty going on all year round. From here we join the South West Coast Path, passing the lifeboat station, home to the lifeboat *Rose*, and Bass Point lookout station.

Bass Point is a fascinating place staffed by volunteers; visitors are welcome to take in the views, learn about Guglielmo Marconi's early 20th-century experiments in transatlantic wireless communication, and chat with the watchkeeper, as long as an incident isn't ongoing.

Continuing along the coast path we round the headland at Lizard Point; the lighthouse here is one of the largest in the world and is open to the public over the summer. Keep an eye out for seals, which can often be seen hauled out on the rocks that edge the coves and beaches. Further west we explore Kynance Cove, a maze of wave-washed boulders strewn across a sandy beach. Our final section heads inland, up and over Lizard Downs, a National Nature Reserve, to return to Lizard village.

AROUND LIZARD POINT

DISTANCE: 13.5KM/8.4 MILES » **TOTAL ASCENT**: 520M/1,706FT » **START GR**: SW 703125 » **TIME**: ALLOW 4.5 HOURS **SATNAV**: TR12 7NQ » **MAP**: OS EXPLORER 103, THE LIZARD, 1:25,000 » **REFRESHMENTS**: ANN'S PASTIES, LIZARD VILLAGE » **NAVIGATION**: VERY SIMPLE COAST PATH AND INLAND LANES AND FOOTPATHS » **BOOK**: *DAY WALKS IN CORNWALL* BY JEN & SIM BENSON.

Lower Predannack Do

Pengersick

Kynance Farm

Ford

Gersick-an-awn

Ogo Pons

5 Soap Rock

Cave

Gew-graze

Pigeon Ogo

Ford

OR

Cave

Settlement

The Horse

Ford

The Pound

Cairn Kynance Cliff

Rill Point

The Rill

Tor Balk

Rill Ledges

Nantivet Rock

Rill Cove

The Bellows

FB

FB

4 Caves

Asparagus Island

Kynance Cove

3

Gull Rock

The Bishop

Lion Rock

LIZARD POINT © JEN & SIM BENSON

16 Around Lizard Point

Directions – Around Lizard Point

➲ **Turn left** (east) out of the car park in the centre of Lizard village and follow Beacon Terrace and then Church Cove Road to the coast at Church Cove. **Turn right** here on to the South West Coast Path (SWCP) and follow it south, passing the lifeboat station to reach Bass Point lookout station. The route now follows the signed SWCP until point **5**. Continue along the clifftop path past the Housel Bay Hotel. The path drops down to the left and across a small footbridge and then continues along the cliff, passing the Lizard Lighthouse and reaches a small car park, cafe and gallery at the road.

2 Continue on the coast path, following the road uphill for a few metres before **turning left** past Polpeor Cove and around Lizard Point. Follow the coast around north and then west until you reach the viewpoint above Kynance Cove, halfway through the walk at around 7.5km.

3 At Kynance Cove, **drop down to join the National Trust path to the beach**. There are two paths here: stay left if the tide is low and drop straight down on to the beach, or if the tide is in stay right and follow the slightly longer path around to the beach by the old buildings.

4 Cross the stream over a bridge and continue along the coast path out along Kynance Cliff to The Rill and then north until you reach a valley with a stream, waterfalls and a path heading inland to the right.

> **OR** In winter, or if it's very wet, the following section is more stream than path. If you'd prefer to avoid wet feet we recommend returning to Kynance Cove via the SWCP and then following the road from the car park to point **6** (GR SW 693131) where you can rejoin the main route and follow the footpath back to the start.

5 Cross the stream and **turn right**, leaving the SWCP and following the path inland to reach a junction of paths near Jolly Town Farm. Turn on to the **right-hand** track, cross the stream and follow the track south between fields to reach a gate. **Turn left** here following the Natural England footpath south-east across Lizard Downs and crossing another stream via a bridge, then **turn right** and head uphill to the National Trust Kynance Cove car park. **Turn left** just before the car park and follow a path across the moorland to reach a lane.

6 **Continue** in the same direction for a short distance, then cross the lane just after the house and use the stile to join a footpath heading south-east across a field and some scrubby moorland to some trees, **ignoring** tracks to the left and right. **Continue** in the same direction through the trees and climb up on to an interesting path that walks along the top of a wall between fields emerging behind a shed in Lizard village. **Turn left** on to the road and follow this back to the start.

SERPENTINITE ROCK, LIZARD © JEN & SIM BENSON

Section 3

Wales

There is some outstanding and diverse walking to be had in Wales. In the north, the rocky peaks and bubbling waterfalls of Snowdonia draw the crowds; to the south the rolling hills of the Brecon Beacons and the delightful coastline of Pembrokeshire are deservedly popular.

CWM LLAFAR, SNOWDONIA © TOM HUTTON

CASCADES ON THE AFON GOCH © TOM HUTTON

17 The Northern Carneddau & Aber Falls, Snowdonia

17km/10.6 miles

A remote expedition over Snowdonia's northernmost summits.

Bont Newydd » Afon Goch » Foel-fras » Carnedd Gwenllian » Bera Bach » Aber Falls » Bont Newydd

Start

Aber Falls car park (parking charge), Bont Newydd. GR: SH 663719.

The Walk

The northern peaks of the Carneddau are quite different to the main summits just a little further south. Whereas Carnedd Llewelyn and Carnedd Dafydd, the two highest mountains in the range, are joined by a narrow, airy ridge that dips deeply into a broad dividing col; the tops of Foel-fras and Carnedd Gwenllian are kept apart by a broad grassy shoulder that falls less than 50 metres from either. This shouldn't put anyone off though – this is still very high ground and it's an exhilarating place to walk.

This is an outing of contrasts, starting close to one of the area's biggest tourist draws – Aber Falls – and then breaking away into something resembling a true wilderness beyond. The crowds are soon left behind and the initial clamber alongside the banks of the beautiful tumbling Afon Goch will almost certainly be a lonely affair.

It gets rougher the higher you get, and most will be relieved when they finally stumble upon a semblance of a path as they reach the spine of the ridge proper. It's then an easy task to link the two summits before starting on the descent. The grand finale is a visit to Aber Falls – a true spectacle in spate.

Incidentally, Carnedd Gwenllian is a recently adopted name for the mountain previously known as Garnedd Uchaf. Gwenllian was the daughter of the last prince of an independent Wales, Llywelyn ap Gruffydd, and his wife Eleanor, after whom Carnedd Llewelyn and Yr Elen are named. Carnedd Dafydd is named after Llywelyn's brother. It's certainly a more fitting title for Snowdonia's 14th highest peak than Garnedd Uchaf, which translates to 'highest cairn'.

THE NORTHERN CARNEDDAU & ABER FALLS

DISTANCE: 17KM/10.6 MILES » **TOTAL ASCENT**: 970M/3,182FT » **START GR**: SH 663719 » **TIME**: ALLOW 6-7 HOURS **SATNAV**: LL33 0LP » **MAP**: OS EXPLORER OL17, SNOWDON, 1:25,000 » **REFRESHMENTS**: CAFFI HEN FELIN AND ABER FALLS CAFE, ABERGWYNGREGYN » **NAVIGATION**: STRAIGHTFORWARD BUT SOME TRACKLESS GOING ON INITIAL ASCENT AND ALSO ON THE DESCENT FROM CARNEDD GWENLLIAN » **BOOK**: DAY WALKS IN SNOWDONIA BY TOM HUTTON.

BERA MAWR AND THE AFON GOCH © TOM HUTTON

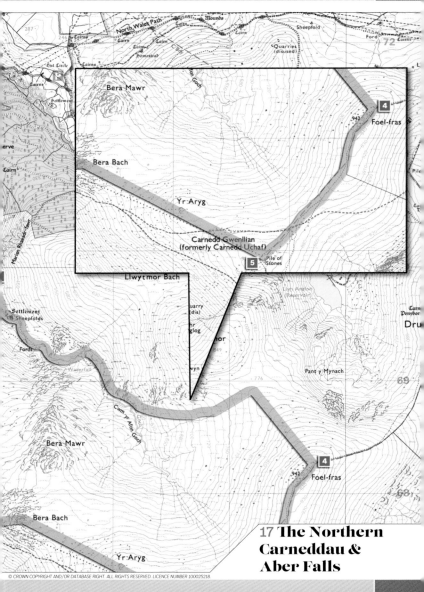

17 The Northern Carneddau & Aber Falls

Directions – The Northern Carneddau & Aber Falls

➲ Go through the gate and follow the main track upstream and over the bridge, where it then merges with a track. **Bear right** on to this to continue uphill to a fork, where you take the **left turn**, signed *Aber Falls*, through the wood. Follow this until it emerges from the wood and then keep **straight ahead** over a ladder stile, where the main path to the falls now drops to the right.

2 **Continue straight ahead** to follow a clear path that traverses the steep slope before continuing along an exposed section, high above the stream. Now follow this, always with the stream on your right, until it eventually levels slightly and enters the remote Cwm yr Afon Goch.

3 Ahead now are the rocky summits of Llwytmor to the left and Bera Mawr to the right. Continue ever upwards, hugging the stream bank as tight as possible until, after passing above a lovely gorge, you **bear half left** to freelance your way up the grassy hillside to a saddle between Llwytmor and Foel-fras. Once in the saddle, **bear right** to the trig point atop Foel-fras (942m).

4 Continue alongside the wall (**heading south-west**) and you'll drop into a shallow dip before climbing easily again to the summit of Carnedd Gwenllian (926m). The jumbled rocks of the summit make a good place to take a breather before moving on.

5 Now leave the main path, which heads towards Foel Grach, and head **north-west**, where you'll pick up a faint path that leads over the rocky tor of Yr Aryg to the next tor – Bera Bach. Continue **west** to pick up a good track that heads directly into the saddle beyond the rugged hilltop of Drosgl.

6 Continue into this saddle and pass beneath the summit before continuing **north-west** towards another saddle; this one at the foot of Moel Wnion. Continue across the floor of the saddle until you pass the head of the Afon Gam and then **bear right** to follow intermittent paths downstream, keeping the waterway to your right the whole time.

7 At the bottom of the descent, you need to cross the stream and continue to a ladder stile that gives access to a good path that will now carry you east to Aber Falls. From here, cross the bridge and follow the track back down to the car park.

FOEL-FRAS © TOM HUTTON

18 Moel Siabod, Snowdonia 19km/11.8 miles

A devious, lonely approach to one of Snowdonia's shapeliest peaks.

Dolwyddelan » Llyn y Foel » Daear Ddu » Carnedd Moel Siabod » Bwlch Rhiw'r Ychen » Carnedd y Cribau » Bwlch y Rhediad » Blaenau Dolwyddelan » Dolwyddelan Castle » Dolwyddelan

Start

Crossroads in the centre of Dolwyddelan. On-street parking or Dolwyddelan Station car park. GR: SH 734524.

The Walk

What Moel Siabod, or just plain 'Siabod' as it's often referred to, lacks in height, it more than makes up for in majesty; especially when viewed from Capel Curig, where it is surely one of Snowdonia's most shapely peaks.

Capel Curig also supplies the starting point for most trade routes up the mountain, but their popularity, and the resulting well-worn paths, seem somewhat out of character with the rest of the Moelwynion range, of which Siabod reigns supreme. So an approach from the south seems somewhat more fitting.

The walk gets off to an ominous start, but the rough pasture soon gives way to easy woodland walking and this in turn leads into a wonderful, secluded cwm.

Steep walking leads to the lovely Llyn y Foel, and from here the airy ridge of Daear Ddu offers easy scrambling almost all the way to the summit. This far, the action has been centred on the better defined face of the Moelwynion, but as height is lost, so the wilder, more remote side of this great massif is revealed and the path that leads south along the ridge is a shining example of everything that's great about walking here.

Another climb gains the wonderfully wild Carnedd y Cribau – this really does feel like the heart of the range – and then it's down to Bwlch y Rhediad to begin your descent. This is surprisingly easy, following soft ground and good tracks. But it's not quite all over yet; there's still a visit to the impressive castle for those that enjoy their history.

MOEL SIABOD

DISTANCE: 19KM/11.8 MILES » **TOTAL ASCENT**: 990M/3,248FT » **START GR**: SH 734524 » **TIME**: ALLOW 7–8 HOURS **SATNAV**: LL25 0EJ » **MAP**: OS EXPLORER OL17, SNOWDON, AND OL18, HARLECH, PORTHMADOG & Y BALA, 1:25,000 **REFRESHMENTS**: GWYDYR HOTEL AND SPAR SHOP (SELLS HOT DRINKS), DOLWYDDELAN » **NAVIGATION**: A CHALLENGING ROUTE WITH SOME UNTRACKED SECTIONS. CARE IS NEEDED TO LOCATE THE RIGHT PATH UP TO LLYN Y FOEL, AND AGAIN TO MAKE SURE THE RIGHT TRAIL IS FOLLOWED DOWN FROM THE SUMMIT. ALTHOUGH THERE'S ONLY FAINT PATHS FOR THE LATTER PART, THERE AREN'T TOO MANY OTHER OPTIONS TO CONFUSE THINGS » **BOOK**: *DAY WALKS IN SNOWDONIA* BY TOM HUTTON.

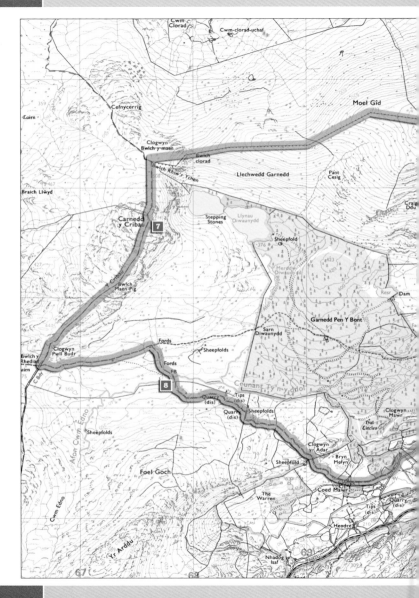

18 **Moel Siabod**

Directions – Moel Siabod

➊ From the main crossroads in the village, keep the Gwydyr Hotel to your right, and the toilets to your left, and walk up the hill. Continue around to the **right**, on to a track, and then **bear left** through a kissing gate on to a footpath. Walk diagonally across the field to another gate and go through this before turning **left** to follow a very boggy path through rough ground with a house to the right.

2 Keep **straight ahead**, following occasional waymarks, and you'll eventually swing **left** over a stile. Turn **immediately right** and follow the field edge into a corner and then continue up to a step stile. Cross this and continue along the line of a tumbledown wall to another stile that leads into the forest. Cross the bridge and follow the path up to join a main forest track where you **turn left**.

3 Follow this track past a few junctions until a waymark directs you **left** on to another major forest track. Follow this around to the **right** to its end, where you cross a bridge and continue on a narrow and rough path that leads into the woods. Follow this up past a waterfall and out on to open ground.

4 Now keep the stream to your left to walk directly uphill and, where the path leaves the stream, below more waterfalls, keep **straight ahead** to climb steeply to the rocky shores of Llyn y Foel. **Turn left** to follow the moraine bank towards the foot of the obvious rocky ridge of Daear Ddu.

5 Once at the foot of the ridge, keep **straight ahead** to walk up on to it, keeping to the left of the initial steep ground and then **bearing right** to join the crest. Now enjoy easy scrambling until it eventually runs out in a deep notch close to the summit. Continue upwards on a rocky path but keep an eye open for a chance to head back right again as there's another short scramble to be enjoyed before you finally reach the trig point.

6 From the summit, head **west** to a stile over a fence and continue over a rocky knoll and down into Bwlch Rhiw'r Ychen. Now follow the fence to another stile, and cross this to climb steeply on to Carnedd y Cribau, which is crowned with a small pool.

7 **Keep ahead** to drop into the next saddle of Bwlch y Rhediad, where a stile on the **left** gives access to a boggy path that leads down into the expanses of Cwm Edno. Follow this across the hillside and pass a ruined building on the right before **turning right** on to a faint and boggy path that drops down to a flagstone bridge over a stream.

8 Cross this and climb to a stile that leads on to a broad track. **Turn left** on to this and follow it for some distance, rounding the foot of Yr Arddu and continuing through a couple of gates to pass through Coed Mawr Farm. Continue to a junction with a small lane and **turn left** on to this to follow it past houses and on up to the farm at Pen-y-rhiw.

9 **Turn left** on to a waymarked track and follow this up, keeping **right** at a fork at the top. Now continue over the hill and down past the remains of Dolwyddelan Castle and keep ahead the whole time to eventually join the main road. **Turn left** to walk easily back into the village.

MOEL SIABOD FROM CAPEL CURIG © TOM HUTTON

SUGAR LOAF FROM YSGYRYD FAWR © ADAM LONG

19 The Sugar Loaf & Crug Mawr, 19.8km/12.3 miles Brecon Beacons

Two splendid tops and a hidden treasure in the heart of the Black Mountains.

Bettws/Forest Coal Pit » Sugar Loaf » Llanbedr » Crug Mawr » Partrishow » Coed-y-Cerrig »
Bettws/Forest Coal Pit

Start

Small parking area on the minor road between Bettws and Forest Coal Pit. GR: SO 292200.

The Walk

The Sugar Loaf is a popular mountain most commonly tackled from the south. Approaching from the north-east, we avoid the crowds and are able to incorporate another fine peak, Crug Mawr, into our walk. Between these two upland sections, we cross peaceful river valleys, pass an astonishingly well-preserved medieval church, and follow boardwalks through a diverse and ancient wood. While at times demanding, this is a walk that demonstrates more than any other the tranquillity and varied beauty of the Black Mountains.

We begin from a small parking area off the minor road between Bettws and Forest Coal Pit. A lovely path climbs steadily to the rocky summit of the Sugar Loaf, where there are fantastic views across a wide area of the Brecon Beacons National Park and the Usk Valley.

Descending westwards, we drop to the Grwyne Fawr and Grwyne Fechan, two sparkling streams whose wooded banks provide delightful walking. A visit to The Red Lion in the pretty village of Llanbedr is also a possibility.

The second big climb crosses Crug Mawr to St Ishow's Church in Partrishow. Once the big climbs are over, we still have to cross the shoulder of hill between Partrishow and Coed-y-Cerrig, a National Nature Reserve of diverse woodland. Boardwalks provide a dry and easy route across the marshy valley bottom. A final climb from Coed-y-Cerrig takes us past the outskirts of Forest Coal Pit and back to our starting point.

THE SUGAR LOAF & CRUG MAWR

DISTANCE: 19.8KM/12.3 MILES » **TOTAL ASCENT**: 914M/2,999FT » **START GR**: SO 292200 » **TIME**: ALLOW 6.5 HOURS
SATNAV: NP7 7LH » **MAP**: OS EXPLORER OL13, BRECON BEACONS NATIONAL PARK: EASTERN AREA, 1:25,000
REFRESHMENTS: THE RED LION, LLANBEDR; NEAREST OTHER PUB IS THE CROWN, PANTYGELLI » **NAVIGATION**: EASY
TO FOLLOW IN FINE WEATHER » **BOOK**: *DAY WALKS IN THE BRECON BEACONS* BY HARRI ROBERTS.

19 The Sugar Loaf & Crug Mawr

Directions – The Sugar Loaf & Crug Mawr

➲ From the car park, take an enclosed path on to the common signed *Sugar Loaf*. **Bear left** along the common edge and begin to climb. Follow the boundary wall as it curves right and climb to a path junction by a wall corner. **Turn left** for about 200m, still following the wall. Just before the path dips, **fork right** and ascend to a spur. Follow the obvious path towards the Sugar Loaf. At a path crossroads below the summit, keep **straight ahead** to clamber up the last few metres to the top.

2 Pass the trig point and cross a jumble of rock. Once off the top, follow a wide grassy path along the mountain's west spur. **Fork right three times** (the last two times in quick succession) and descend steeply to a wide grassy path contouring around the base of the hill. Cross the path and follow a fence down to a rusty metal gate. A grassy bridleway descends from here to a rough vehicle track. **Turn left** and descend gently to a farm.

3 Follow a lane downhill to the next footpath **on the right**. Waymarks lead across fields to a track in front of Gellyrhydd Farm. **Turn left**, then **right** at the next track, signed *Pen-y-bont*. Take the next footpath **on the left** and descend to a footbridge across the Grwyne Fawr river. Cross a field towards a gate, keeping the smaller Grwyne Fechan river to your left. Cross a lane and another field, and climb on to a shoulder of land above the river. A rough track drops back down to the river. Continue upstream as far as the second bridge on the left.

4 **Turn right** on to a zigzagging path up the side of the wooded valley (or left over the bridge if you wish to detour to Llanbedr). Where the path divides, **fork left** and climb steeply. Continue along a field edge and cross a lane. After a second field, **aim left** of a house and join a track. At a waymark, **turn left** up a steep slope and climb to a junction with a bridleway.

5 **Turn left** and follow a sunken track through woodland to a gate on to the mountain. Follow the common boundary uphill until a sharp right turn. Keep **straight ahead** for a short distance, then **bear right**. The path briefly rejoins the common edge, then **bears left** below the higher ground of Blaen yr Henbant. Continue along the main path above Cwm Milaid as far as a *Beacons Way* marker at the head of the valley. **Turn right**, in the direction of the arrow, and climb a short, steep slope to the summit of Crug Mawr.

6   Keep **straight ahead** in the direction of a *Beacons Way* arrow. After a pond, the path descends more steeply. **Bear left** near the bottom of the common, keeping a fence to your right. **Fork right** to continue along the fence and descend to a dry-stone wall. **Turn right** and pass through two gates on to a rough enclosed track. Keep **straight ahead** on to a lane and soon after begin to descend steeply.

7   At a sign for *St Ishow's Church*, **turn left** through a metal gate and descend between gravestones. **Turn left** past the church (which is kept open for visitors) and continue through a kissing gate into a field. Keep **straight ahead** to a wall corner above a farmhouse and **turn sharp right**, following the wall downhill to a metal gate. **Turn left** between farm buildings. At the end of the house, **bear left** through a rusty farm gate into a field.

8   Follow *Beacons Way* markers down through fields and past a stone ruin. **Bear left** on to a rough track and drop to a lane. Take the narrow lane opposite signed *Tabernacle Chapel* and cross the Grwyne Fawr river. Leave the Beacons Way by **turning right** on to a lane.

9   Continue past a house on to a grassy track. Climb steadily along the side of the valley to reach another house. Pass behind the house and **keep straight ahead** along the access track. At a lane, **keep straight ahead** across a stone stile opposite and follow the right edge of a field to another stone stile. Cross a track below a small quarry on to a rough track opposite.

10   Cross a road in front of a grand house and join a track below the buildings. Follow a grassy track down to a lake and drop to a stile into woods. Descend through trees, **bearing right** along the main path to a small parking area. Cross a road and join a boardwalk above the marshy valley bottom. Take either fork where the path splits, both branches rejoining. At a rough track, **turn right** and climb back across the wooded slope.

11   At a T-junction with a wider track, **turn right** and follow the track downhill to a lane. **Turn left** at the next vehicle track, signed *Bettws*. Keep ahead at a house on to a short section of grassy track into a field. Follow the left-hand edge, then **aim right**, down to a metal gate in the bottom corner. Join a rough, boggy track along the valley bottom, climbing higher up the bank if this is waterlogged. **Keep straight ahead** at a lane and climb to a T-junction. **Turn right** and walk for about 150m to return to the car park.

LOOKING EAST ALONG THE COAST FROM NEAR WEST HOOK FARM © ADAM LONG

20 St Brides & the Marloes Peninsula, Pembrokeshire Coast

16.5km/10.3 miles

Island views along Pembrokeshire's Atlantic coast.

St Brides » Musselwick Sands » Martin's Haven » Wooltack Point » Marloes Sands » Marloes »
St Brides

Start
**National park car park at St Brides.
GR: SM 802109.**

The Walk
There is something magical about the far west of Pembrokeshire and the coastal scenery around Marloes is some of the most spectacular in the national park. Our route begins with a wonderful stretch of coast path, taking us west from St Brides past Musselwick Sands and on to Martin's Haven, the small harbour where in spring and summer visitors embark for Skomer Island.

The view from Wooltack Point, at the far western end of the so-called 'Deer Park', is the next best thing to visiting the island itself. From here the eastern tip of Skomer Island is little more than a kilometre away, with the smaller Midland Isle being less than half that. The islands are best known for their seabirds and contain internationally important colonies of puffin and Manx shearwater. The surrounding seas are equally rich in wildlife and are one of only three designated marine nature reserves in the UK.

After rounding the headland, open cliffs lead us past Gateholm Island and behind the beautiful Marloes Sands. To the south-west, there are good views of Skokholm Island, slightly lower in the water than its counterpart to the north.

Leaving the coast, we head inland towards Marloes. The main route described bypasses the centre of the village, but it is worth making the detour if only to see the splendid clock tower built as a memorial to the 4th Baron Kensington. The baron was well known locally as the tenant of St Brides Castle, a 19th-century baronial-style house now converted into luxury holiday apartments. Field paths between Marloes and St Brides take us directly below the 'castle', which sits on a low hill above the bay.

ST BRIDES & THE MARLOES PENINSULA
DISTANCE: 16.5KM/10.3 MILES » **TOTAL ASCENT**: 496M/1,627FT » **START GR**: SM 802109 » **TIME**: ALLOW 5.5 HOURS
SATNAV: SA62 3AJ » **MAP**: OS EXPLORER OL36, SOUTH PEMBROKESHIRE, 1:25,000 » **REFRESHMENTS**: THE LOBSTER POT INN AND THE CLOCK HOUSE, MARLOES » **NAVIGATION**: EASY AND WELL MARKED » **BOOK**: *DAY WALKS ON THE PEMBROKESHIRE COAST* BY HARRI ROBERTS.

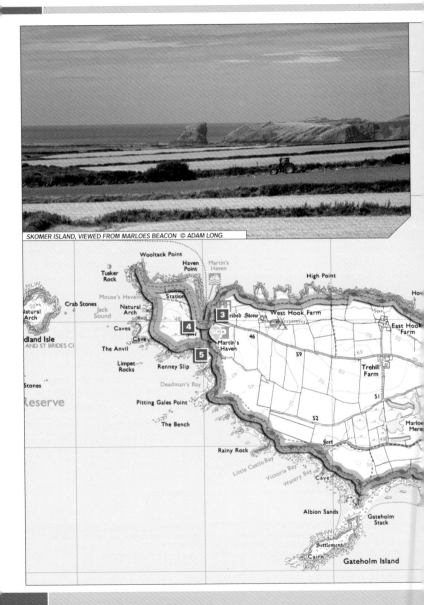

SKOMER ISLAND, VIEWED FROM MARLOES BEACON © ADAM LONG

20 St Brides & the Marloes Peninsula

Directions – St Brides & the Marloes Peninsula

⊛ Walk past St Brides Church towards a gap in a stone wall. Pass through the gap, following a coast path sign for *Martin's Haven*. Continue through a picnic area and along a field edge, the former estate boundary wall to your right. Shortly leave the field and join a clifftop path, the boundary wall now to your left. Follow the cliffs as far as Musselwick Sands (around 3.7km).

2 After descending to an access point behind the beach, the path climbs inland to the left for around 100m. **Ignore** the path continuing ahead and **turn sharply right** to return to the coastal cliffs. Continue along a clear clifftop path for a further 2.9km to reach the small pebbly bay of Martin's Haven.

> ↪ For a shorter walk, take the path **continuing ahead** inland from Musselwick. **Turn left** at a road and rejoin the main route after point **7** on the outskirts of Marloes.

3 Join the road climbing **to the left**, past toilets and the Skomer Marine Nature Reserve office. At the top of the hill, **turn right** through a gate in a wall and climb straight up the grassy slope ahead.

> ↪ The circuit around the Deer Park can be omitted by **turning left** immediately after the gate and following the official coast path parallel to the wall. Rejoin the main route at Renney Slip (point **5**).

4 At the top of the steps, **fork right** towards a white wooden hut (an automatic weather station) on a hill. **Bear slightly left** from the hut and descend towards the cliffs immediately opposite Midland Isle and Skomer Island. For the best island views, **turn right** and follow the path up to a level grassy platform above Wooltack Point. Retrace your steps and follow the cliffs round to rejoin the official coast path at Renney Slip.

5 The coast path continues across open grassy cliffs towards Gateholm Island. **Bear right** at the end of the large open area to continue alongside a fence. Once past the 'island', the path **bears left**, above the long curve of Marloes Sands.

6 Soon after climbing a short flight of steps, leave the coast path by **turning left** at a *footpath* sign. Go through a gate and follow a clear grassy path along the right-hand edge of two fields to a T-junction with a track. **Turn right**, passing toilets and a number of converted farm buildings (the former Marloes Sands youth hostel), and reach a junction with a road. **Turn right.**

7 About 750m after joining the road, and just past Marloes Court on the right, **turn left** into a field at a *footpath* sign. Follow the right-hand field boundary ahead until you emerge on a road to the left of a pink house. **Turn right** and enter the village of Marloes. Take the first track **on the left** then immediately **turn right** on to another track.

> **OR** For The Lobster Pot Inn and The Clock House, continue along the road into the centre of Marloes. To rejoin the main route, take the road opposite The Lobster Pot, past the public toilets and up to a house called The Fold. Join a path **to the left** of the entrance and emerge in a field. **Keep ahead** along the **left-hand** field edge to a junction with a track and **turn right**.

8 The track ends at a house called The Old School. **Keep ahead** through a kissing gate and follow the path along the left-hand edge of two fields. Shortly after entering a third field, with Fopston Farm across the field to the right, cross a stile **on the left** and join a track. **Turn right** and descend to a track junction in a dip. **Turn right.**

9 Take the second signed path **on the left**, just before a junction with a lane. Follow the right-hand edge of four fields, bypassing the old stone stiles via woodland gates **on the right**. Keep **straight ahead** across a track and then the access road to St Brides Castle. Cross a field towards St Brides Church and walk through the churchyard to the car park.

Appendix

USEFUL WEBSITES

www.breconbeacons.org
www.cotswolds.com
www.highweald.org
www.lakedistrict.gov.uk
www.northyorkmoors.org.uk
www.peakdistrict.gov.uk
www.pembrokeshirecoast.wales
www.southdowns.gov.uk
www.southpennines.co.uk
www.visitcornwall.com
www.visitdevon.co.uk
www.visitnorfolk.co.uk
www.visitnorthumberland.com
www.visitsnowdonia.info
www.yorkshiredales.org.uk

WEATHER

www.metoffice.gov.uk
www.mwis.org.uk

OTHER PUBLICATIONS

Big Trails: Great Britain & Ireland
Edited by Kathy Rogers and Stephen Ross,
Vertebrate Publishing
www.v-publishing.co.uk

Big Trails: Great Britain & Ireland Volume 2
Edited by Kathy Rogers and Stephen Ross,
Vertebrate Publishing
www.v-publishing.co.uk

South Downs Way Guidemap
Vertebrate Publishing
www.v-publishing.co.uk

Hadrian's Wall Path Guidemap
Vertebrate Publishing
www.v-publishing.co.uk

The Beaches of Wales
Alistair Hare, Vertebrate Publishing
www.v-publishing.co.uk

THE OLD KEIGHLEY ROAD ACROSS ILKLEY MOOR, SOUTH PENNINES © PAUL BESLEY

"Raise the **weather Forcefield!**"

Day Walks Guidebooks

Written by local authors, each pocket-sized guidebook features:

Map data

- 20 great day-length walks
- Ordnance Survey 1:25,000-scale maps
- easy-to-follow directions
- distance & navigation information
- refreshment stops & local area information
- detailed appendix

Available from book shops or direct from:
www.v-publishing.co.uk

ABOUT THE EDITOR

Jon Barton is the founder of Vertebrate Publishing, Britain's number one publisher of outdoor activity and adventure books. He's the author of Vertebrate's bestselling *Peak District Mountain Biking* and *White Peak Mountain Biking* guides, as well as climbing and trail running guidebooks to the Peak District. A keen runner, climber, mountain biker and fell walker, Jon has a huge amount of experience travelling the world in search of adventures, but loves coming home to Sheffield and the Peak District where his favourite adventures always start.

VERTEBRATE PUBLISHING

At Vertebrate Publishing we publish books to inspire adventure.

It's our rule that the only books we publish are those that we'd want to read or use ourselves. We endeavour to bring you beautiful books that stand the test of time and that you'll be proud to have on your bookshelf for years to come.

The Peak District was the inspiration behind our first books. Our offices are situated on its doorstep, minutes away from world-class climbing, biking and hillwalking. We're driven by our own passion for the outdoors, for exploration, and for the natural world; it's this passion that we want to share with our readers.

We aim to inspire everyone to get out there. We want to connect readers – young and old – with the outdoors and the positive impact it can have on well-being. We think it's particularly important that young people get outside and explore the natural world, something we support through our publishing programme.

As well as publishing award-winning new books, we're working to make available many out-of-print classics in both print and digital formats. These are stories that we believe are unique and significant; we want to make sure that they continue to be shared and enjoyed. *www.v-publishing.co.uk*